Ponderings from My PORCH SWING

Ponderings from My
PORCH
SWING

PEGGY PURCELL HANNA

XULON PRESS

Xulon Press
2301 Lucien Way #415
Maitland, FL 32751
407.339.4217
www.xulonpress.com

Printed in the United States of America.

Paperback ISBN-13: 978-1-63221-236-8

eBook ISBN-13: 978-1-6322-1237-5

Ahh-the Porch Swing...

where wisdom and sharing flow freely and safely
* a successful recipe
*a deepening friendship
*the joys and heartaches of raising children

where the tranquil view gives a sense of well-being and hope for a
peaceful future
*a gentle rocking
*a good friend
*encouragement from Scripture

where all are welcome at any time
*sit back
*relax
*enjoy some sage insights from a porch-swing ponderer.

Written by my dear swing-sharing friend, Katie

Table of Contents

A Basket Case

Not long ago, I heard someone who was going through a very trying period in her life say these words, "I'm just a *basket case.*"

I knew exactly what she meant. How many times have I used that very phrase when my world has been turned upside down, and my life has been in turmoil? While pondering this thought, God interrupted, "My child, you aren't looking at those words from My point of view. It's a *good* thing to be a *basket case.*"

"A *good* thing?" I exclaimed.

"Yes," He continued, "Moses was a *basket case* and so was Paul."

"What do You mean they were *basket cases?*"

"Well, dear one, they were experiencing very severe trials in their lives, and I used *baskets* to deliver them both. So, remember, when you feel as if you are a *basket case*, it's a *good* thing. *You are about to be delivered!*"

> Holy Spirit, I finally see,
> Within Your *basket*, all doubts flee.
> I wait in peace; You deliver me!
> A *basket case* is good to be!!

Lord, when I'm facing adversity and experiencing the "last straw," please help me jump into Your basket of safety and relax in peace, full of assurance that deliverance is near because You know exactly what to do with **basket cases***!*

If you will indulge me, I would like to assure you that the preceding words have not been written by someone who has never known sorrow, pain, heartache, fear, or hopelessness. I may not have been through the same storms you have walked through, but I do know what it feels like to be wet.

At the age of 16, I lost my father to pancreatic cancer.

After many years of marriage, I found myself a heart-broken, single mother with three young children, no job, and no money.

I watched my younger daughter struggle through two heart surgeries. Her first was at five months and her second, which was open-heart surgery, was at eight years of age. I later saw her walk through the same heart-wrenching, emotional path I had traveled as she watched her four-year old son, my grandson, go through open-heart surgery.

I witnessed my older daughter experience two miscarriages and then labor for hours knowing that the tiny baby she would soon cradle in her arms for only fleeting moments had, the day before, already passed into the arms of God. A few years later I saw her come within days of death before finally being diagnosed with Adison's disease.

I broken-heartedly watched my son and daughter walk through the deaths of their spouses, one to a long, drawn-out battle with cancer and one to a devastating car accident.

I cared for my precious mother in our home for years as she bravely fought through six cancer surgeries and blindness.

I stood by my beloved husband's hospital bed after a heart attack as he battled for two months repeatedly on and off ventilators, not knowing if the next day would bring life or death.

These are some of my life's experiences I share with you to simply say this: I have faced many *basket case* situations, but, like Moses and Paul, God has always been there with His *basket* to deliver me. I truly know that I can trust Him through any trial the enemy throws at me because God knows exactly what to do with **basket cases**!

A Peanut Butter and Jelly Sandwich

I have been pondering and have come to the conclusion that perhaps I look a little like a peanut butter and jelly sandwich to God. Actually, make that a peanut butter and grape jelly sandwich because I love the taste of plump, purple grapes. Therefore, because it is my heart's desire to live up to the image God has of me, I want to strive to taste and look like a picture-perfect PBJ concoction.

But, just like a peanut butter and jelly sandwich can be a little messy in the assembling process, I too, in trying to look and taste good for God can be a little messy in the preparation procedure.

I think a PBJ sandwich is an excellent example of my spirit, soul, and body. (Well, maybe not excellent, but pretty good.) I see the bread as a symbol of my spirit in whom Jesus resides. It's the bedrock of the sandwich. After all, Jesus is our Cornerstone, our Bread of Life; and without Him as the foundation nothing else really matters.

The peanut butter is my soul (my mind, will, and emotions) some-times getting me in sticky situations, sometimes smoothing out the rough spots in my life, and sometimes making me a little nutty. Too much peanut butter causes dryness. If all I have to offer others is my own soulish wisdom and emotional stability, I'm going to be pretty dry and difficult to swallow at times.

The grape jelly represents my flesh, the part the world sees, the part that adds sweetness, fun, and zest. But alas, sometimes I put too much jelly in one place. It's clumpy, overwhelming in fact, too much sweetness in one bite. It's rather like me trying to be too spiritual, quoting too much scripture, being so "heavenly minded that I'm no earthly good." Then there's the other problem. If the grapes aren't ripe or not enough sugar has been added…well, can you say, "Sour grapes"? All the sweetness has disappeared.

I know that sometimes, like peanut butter and jelly being spread on too thick, I come on too strong, too full of self, too pretentious, too prideful. I don't allow the substance of the Bread to be tasted because I am lifting myself up, trying to "draw all men to me" instead of to Jesus.

*Oh, Lord, teach me how to spread the peanut butter and jelly in just the right amount so the flavor of the Bread comes through, and the world can **taste and see that You are good.***

Beside You, Not Behind

Behind each good man stands a woman,
We've heard the wise men say.
Not behind, but right beside you
Is where she's been each day.

She's shared with you the good times,
The laughter, and the tears.
She has always been beside you
Throughout the passing years.

Whenever you were discouraged,
Whether you smiled or wore a frown,
She was standing there beside you;
She never let you down.

Some think she has been behind you
As you've succeeded throughout life,
But you know she's been beside you.
Your best friend, your lover, your wife.

Genesis 2:21-25

Blooming...Bowing...Blessed

oday when I looked at the beautiful bouquet of birthday roses from my son, I noticed three of them beginning to droop. I always feel a sadness when I see this happen because it signifies the beginning demise of a once-beautiful flower. But as I contemplated their pre-funeral arrangements (a trip to the wastebasket), a gentle thought nudged its way into my mind.

What if I were to look at those flowers from God's perspective?

Suddenly I saw them as God sees them. In His eyes, they weren't drooping, they were bowing; and they were, to Him, even more beautiful now than at the height of their glory.

They were bowing before their Creator in humble worship. They were saying, "Father, we have finished our task, the purpose for which we were created. Our calling was to glorify You by bringing Your beauty and fragrance into the lives of others. Our assignment has been completed. We have accomplished our mission. We have shown forth Your beauty to the world, and the time is drawing near for us to joyfully proclaim: It is finished! Now, Father, we bow before You in humble anticipation, eagerly waiting to hear Your loving, glorious words:

Well done, good and faithful servants. You have run the race. You have fought the good fight. You have glorified My Name. You are blessed. Welcome into My presence!"

I began to ponder why some of the roses had bowed and finished their purpose in life before the others. They were seemingly gone before their time and it didn't seem quite fair.

"That," said God, "was My decision. Their times are in My hands. You need not burden yourself with that question because they are My creation and My servants. I will simply say to you what I said to My beloved Peter long ago: *What is that to you, My child? You concentrate on following Me, and I will take care of them…and you."*

Tears of love, gratitude, and understanding flowed as I closed my eyes and bowed my head. Oh, Father, that I, like these roses, would fix my eyes on You alone and fulfill my calling to glorify You by bringing Your beauty and fragrance into the lives of others. That I would one day stand before You with bowed head and say: It is finished. And I, like them, would hear those sacred words:

Well done, good and faithful servant. You have run the race. You have fought the good fight. You have glorified My Name. You are blessed. Welcome into My presence!

I don't think these roses have quite finished their purpose here on earth. I plan to keep them around just a little longer than usual, so I can soak in the precious beauty and fragrance of their humbly bowed heads as they remind me that my Father doesn't always look at things the way I do.

Boot Camp for Our Babies

D o you have children who are breaking your heart because they are not walking with the Lord? Do they seem to be destroying themselves and the lives of all those who love them? Have you spent sleepless nights worrying? Anxious days praying?

My heart goes out to you and identifies completely. I have walked that path.

As mothers, we would do anything to protect our wayward children, make them happy, and bring them home to God and to us, wouldn't we?

Over the years, God, with love and patience, has taught me this:

Our children are in a war, and we cannot fight their battles for them.

Many of us would gladly go to Iraq or Afghanistan to fight for our sons and daughters if we could; but we know that's impossible. So, how do we help our soldiers in the battle? We do it through prayers and encouraging words written in letters.

Many of us Christian mothers would go into the very pit of hell itself to fight for the souls of our sons and daughters if we could; but that, too, is impossible. So, just how can we help our *prodigal soldiers* in the battle for their eternal lives?

Following are some of the ways I believe Holy Spirit has shown me that we, as Christian mothers, can help our *prodigal* loved ones come through this war victoriously:

*We can bring them, in prayer, to our Father and turn them over to Him. He is the *General*, and He knows the battle plan. He can be trusted with our precious recruits.

*While in prayer, we can bless our children with scriptures we find in the Bible (Read them aloud to God and ourselves).

*Speak God's promises. Declare them aloud to our ears and the ears of the enemy.

*When possible, speak God's words of encouragement to our children, remind them Who they belong to and how much He loves them.

*Remind them of the things they've heard from the *General*, from you, and from others throughout their lives. (No preaching, just gentle, truthful facts stated with the authority God has given us as parents.)

*Do not let the enemy steal that authority from us. It is ours. Take it! Use it when Holy Spirit prompts us to use it. If we don't feel prompted, be still and know that He is God, and He will get His words to them in His way and in His time.

*If we goof up, we must learn to lean back, take a deep breath and say: "Oops, sorry, Father, I forgot for a minute that you are the *General*, and I am Your *foot soldier* following

Your orders and Your plans. You have it all worked out for my children.

I will take my hands and my mind off them and let You, God, bring them to and through Your boot camp."

We must remember: Moms can't go to the world's boot camps with their kids. They have to let go. We can't go to God's boot camp with our kids either, but we know that when we let go, we are letting them go into the very strong, very capable hands of Almighty God Himself. In words, familiar to us, we can *let go and let God.*

Boot Camp is where *boys become men.* It's tough, and it's hard. I'm sure if moms could see what their "babies" have to endure while going through the world's boot camps, they would be horrified and heartbroken; but when those "babies" finally graduate, they are no longer children, but men and women.

It may break our hearts as we watch our "babies" go through God's boot camp, but when they finally graduate, they will no longer be children, but men and women of God!

And isn't this the desire of every Christian mother's heart...to see her children become mighty men and women of our Mighty God?

But Father, I Can't Sing

One day the Father was watching and listening to the song being sung by His children. "Listen," He said to me, "Listen to the song My children are singing. Isn't it beautiful?"

"Oh yes, Father," I answered. "it truly is!"

"And look," He said, "look at the song My children are singing."

"Look?" I questioned. "How can I look at a song? I can listen to a song, but I can't look at one, Father."

"Oh yes you can," He chided gently. "Here, just lean over a little closer to Me. Now look at My comely *HIGH* notes. They reach heights that no one else can. Look. Aren't they beautiful? They stand high above the others, and they touch My Spirit. They love Me very much. Do you see them?"

"Oh yes, Father, they're...they're breath-taking!"

"Yes, they are," He said. "I created them that way, and they bless Me so much."

"Oh, I wish I were a *HIGH* note, Father. I want to bless You."

He smiled.

"Look at My *MIDDLE* notes. See how many there are? See how they run, and jump, and work, and play to make the melodious sounds that touch My very heart? They love Me very much. Do you see them?"

"Oh yes, Father!" I cried. They're...they're so joyful!"

"Yes, they are. I created them that way, and they bless Me so much."

"Oh, I wish I were a *MIDDLE* note, Father. I want to bless You."

Again, He smiled.

"Look at My *LOW* notes. See how calm and steady they are. They reach down into the very depth of their souls to keep the rhythm flowing peacefully in the songs that touch My ears. They love Me very much. Do you see them?"

"Oh yes, Father. They're...they're so peaceful!"

"Yes, they are. I created them that way, and they bless Me so much."

"Oh, I wish I were a *LOW* note, Father. I want to bless You."

Then, with a broken heart, I fell at His feet, weeping bitterly. "Oh, Abba, I love you so much, and I want to bless You, too; but I'm not a *HIGH* note, or a *MIDDLE* note, or a *LOW* note. I can't even carry a tune."

The Father gently lifted me onto His lap, raised my face to His, and spoke, "Oh My little one, I created you exactly the way you are, and you bless Me so much."

"But, Father," I sobbed, "I don't have a *place* in the song Your children sing."

"My child," He whispered tenderly, "your *place* is here beside Me. If you weren't here to look and listen with Me, with whom would I share My songs of joy?"

Clutterbusters for Christians

As Christmas time approaches, I begin thinking about clearing out the clutter in our home to make room for the new clutter that goes with decorating for the holidays. My husband thinks I try to decorate every surface in the house that dares to appear unclaimed. Yes, I even decorate my porch. I say, "Hey! Can I help it if I have so many Christmas baubles that delight my heart with pleasant memories?" So, I begin my yearly de-cluttering frenzy.

Now over my lifetime I have read hundreds of articles (well, maybe not hundreds, but a big bunch) describing the best way to clear clutter. I decided that perhaps now would be a good time to put some of those tips into practice. As I was pondering over which one I should begin practicing, I felt Holy Spirit gently tapping on my spiritual shoulder. "You know," He whispered, "you could do some *clutterbusting* in your soul this season too."

"You're right," I mused. "I have been noticing a few *piles of pride,* some *mountains of moodiness,* and *darkness dust bunnies* in my life lately. Perhaps it would be a good idea to take some of those clutter-clearing rules into my prayer closet and commence *clutterbusting* my heart."

Rule #1 Start with the room you spend the most time in. I need to start spending more time in my prayer room with Jesus. I need to choose each day who it is I want to serve:

my *Self* or my LORD. I think I'll start spending more time focusing on *God's Rules of Order* for my life: praying, reading His word, being thankful, practicing gratitude, and praising Him. This should help get rid of some of the *Self* messes that are cluttering up my life.

Rule #2 Avoid zigzagging and don't try to cover everything all at once. I must face the realization that I am not Holy Spirit Jr. I am not in charge of everyone and everything in my little world. I must stop bouncing from one thing to another, *pinging* as my husband calls it, and wearing myself out trying to do everything at once. I need to practice being still, knowing that He is God, He is in charge, and He is *very* capable of handling *everything*. I must sloooow down.

Rule #3 Attack the visible clutter first. I do need to look closely at my visible sins, but I don't need to focus on them constantly. I need to look at how far God has brought me. I need to concentrate on His love for me and the good things I do. I need to stop being so *Self*-centered and remember the wise words I once read describing how to deal with the feeling of condemnation that tries to attack me when I feel as if I have failed God: "I haven't arrived yet, but I've left." My God Who *began a good work in me will complete it.* He knows who I am and what I'm like, and He still likes me anyway!

Rule #4 Don't Get Distracted. I can't let the enemy distract me. I must focus on Jesus, His love, and His word, and not my circumstances, the devil, or his lies. I need to resist falling into the trap of the *Tyranny of the Urgent* and fix my eyes on the Lord.

Rule #5 Search for and keep the treasures, not the trash. I must look for *God Moments* everywhere. I need to consider (think, ponder, meditate) on those things which are positive, good, honorable, lovely, and worthy; and not on things which are negative, dark, harmful and evil. I must remember that God is good and brings life, and that Satan is evil and brings death and destruction. I must not ascribe evil happenings to God because *every good and perfect gift comes from Him.*

So, this year as I am *clutterbusting* my home in preparation for my Christmas decorations, I think I will continue to think of ways I can *clutterbust* my *Self* in anticipation of celebrating the most good and perfect gift God ever gave...JESUS!

Dark Night of the Soul

Today, my dear friend's husband had to go back on a ventilator after having had an abdominal aortic aneurysm. I was praying for him; and suddenly, my own husband's past experience in hospitals on ventilators overwhelmed me. The emotions came crowding back in on me. Faith seemed to evaporate completely. I had nothing to pray, absolutely nothing to say to God. I could find no words. I felt only a creeping hopelessness that threatened to engulf me in its intensity.

Dark nights of the soul can come at any time without warning, without signs. Or do they really come without warning? Are the signs there, and am I simply unaware of them?

Too preoccupied with life to sense them?

Too secure in my own inept strength?

Too full of my 'self' plans?

Too comfortable leaning on my 'wisdom' from previous encounters with my God?

The reasons matter not. They will soon enough be brought to center-stage in my thoughts for contemplation. What matters most is what I do with this encroaching, invading, enveloping, darkness that threatens to press me, in suffocation, to its breast.

I cry. A release of emotions.

There is a hush in the heavens. All activity ceases. For one split second I am the center of the universe as heavenly beings, both angelic and demonic, wait. Wait in anticipation for my decision.

Faith has fled. Feelings reign. The choice is mine. Where will I turn?

My anguished cry of despair and indecision echoes in the stillness, "Father, I feel overwhelmed! Help me! Oh, how I need faith to come!"

Then miraculously, from somewhere deep within my being, the still, small voice of my God whispers these words, "**Faith comes by hearing...and hearing by the Word of God.**"

The silence reigns. The choices stand. Faith or Feeling? To which will I turn?

Setting my face like flint, I walk determinedly to my Bible, open it, and press His precious, faith-bringing words fiercely and lovingly into my heart as I begin to read.

The heavens sigh. The decision has been made. I have turned. I have chosen faith. The dark night of my soul has fled.

Decisions and Doubts

he School Bell rings. * H.S. School (*Holy Spirit) is now in session.

Today's Lesson: Decisions and Doubts 101. Text: James 1:5-8

Student's Name: Me

The Holy Spirit begins His lecture with these words: "*If anyone lacks wisdom ask God, and He will give it to you, but if you don't ask in faith, you won't get it.* Do you know the meaning of these verses?" He asks.

"Oh yes, I do!" I exclaim.

"Ah," He smiles, "but do you truly believe them?"

"Well, of course I believe them!"

"Do you practice them?"

"Well, ye-es," I answer hesitantly.

"Always?" He queries.

(Deep breath on my part.) "Fairly often," I reply.

"And you're very sure you believe all of them?"

(I ponder a few seconds, then answer confidently) "Yes, yes, I'm very sure."

"Do you mind if we examine your belief more closely?" He asks quietly.

"Well, uh, I guess not."

"Do you remember that big decision you made last week?"

"Ye-es." I nod slowly. (I'm beginning to sense where this might be going.)

"You really prayed about that decision, didn't you?"

"Oh, yes! I really did!"

"Didn't you ask God for wisdom, and then after much pondering, make your decision?"

"Yes. Yes, I did."

"If you really believe that God does what He says He will do, why were you thinking the following thought this morning? *(I wonder if I made the right decision? I thought I did, BUT it LOOKS, SOUNDS, and FEELS as if I didn't.)* Do you believe God's word is true?

"Yes."

"Do you think God is lying when He says, 'Ask Me for wisdom, and I'll give it to you.'?"

"No."

"Did you lack wisdom in the situation, and did you ask for it?"

"Yes."

"Well, if you asked, and if you believe He heard you and is not a liar, BUT you are doubting your decision, then I'm afraid you must be labeled as a BUT-head."

"A BUT-head!!?"

"Yes, a James 1:6 *BUT*-head. You asked, BUT now you have the BUTS sloshing around inside your head: BUT it looks like, BUT it sounds like, BUT it feels like…I made a mistake. From the sound of all those sloshing BUTS, it appears you didn't really ask in faith, and now you are suffering from SEE sickness."

"SEA sickness? You mean like nauseous, throwing up sea sickness?"

"No, I mean S.E.E sickness. You are being tossed around by your SENSES, what you SEE, and what you FEEL. If you are questioning whether or not you made the right decision after asking God for wisdom, then you're LOOKING at the circumstances and letting what you SEE dictate FEELINGS of confusion and doubt to your mind.

You're like an ocean wave being blown about by the wind. You have made your SENSES your gods. You are focusing on them. Your SENSES, not GOD, are controlling your thoughts. So, don't be surprised that you're feeling SEE sick. You are simply *trusting in your* SENSES *with all your heart and leaning upon the understanding of your own* SENSES.. *You are acknowledging your* SENSES *in all your ways, and* THEY *are directing your paths."* (Prov. 3:5,6 paraphrased by me)

Holy Spirit quietly closed the Teacher's Guide, looked directly into my heart, and ended the lesson with this one question, "If you're not going to ask for wisdom with faith, why even bother to ask at all?"

Class dismissed.

Did God Really Say?

I n John 14:30 Jesus says: *Hereafter I will **not talk much** more with you: for the prince of this world is coming, and has nothing in me.* Jesus was talking with those who were closest to Him. He knew He was facing a trial and wanted to prepare them and Himself for it.

While reading these words, the Lord spoke to me: *My child, when you are facing a trial, you need to **not talk much**.* (Meaning I need to watch my words very carefully.) *You must rein in negative words: words of complaint, worry, fear, despair, hopelessness, apathy.* (Those of us who tend to talk much often get ourselves into trouble with our words. Trust me, I know.)

Proverbs 10:19 says: In a multitude of words transgression is not lacking, but he who restrains his lips is wise. (Many of us utter every word that shows up on the rough-copy pages of our brains. We often hit the 'Send' key without proofreading. Then, oops, too late to 'Delete'.)

God continued speaking: *When you are going through a trial, the enemy turns up the volume of his negative suggestions, intimations, innuendos, and taunts until the cacophony of his LIES begin to drown out My Voice. This is the time when it becomes very easy for you to begin to quietly murmur Satan's words aloud. His words contradict every covenant promise I have given you. He spoke the same words thousands of years ago to Eve who was facing the biggest trial of her life. She had to decide to believe My word or his. She heard the same words he still uses to speak to you today: DID GOD REALLY SAY?*

Satan will take every promise you read, every promise you cling to in your time of battle, every promise you are holding tightly onto with your last vestige of strength, and He will tack on those four little words at the end: DID GOD REALLY SAY?

When you see those words on the computer of your brain, you must close your eyes, take a deep breath, whisper the name of Jesus, and type in bold, large font, the word YES! Then hit 'Send.' I have told you in James 4:7 that if you resist the devil, he will flee. You can 'Delete' him. The reason you can type the word YES with certainty is because ALL My promises are YES, in Christ; and so, through Christ, you can say AMEN to them. (This is in I Corinthians.1:20, in case you're interested.) It also says (in Numbers 23:19, Titus 1:1-3, and Hebrews 6:18) that I can't lie. (I'm pretty sure I heard Him chuckle when He gave me all those scripture addresses.)

The last part of John 14:30 tells you how it is possible for you to type YES to those words! It is inevitable that the prince of this world will come after you in some way and at some time; but the four little words at the end of this verse will give you hope. Listen to the words of My Son: 'The prince of this world will come, but he HAS NOTHING IN ME.'

This means: *Satan has no claim on Jesus.
*Satan has nothing in common with Jesus.
*There is nothing in Jesus that belongs to Satan.
*Satan has no power over Jesus.

Therefore, since you have Christ in you, the Hope of Glory, and since you are the righteousness of Me, God, in Christ, and since My Spirit who raised Jesus from the dead is living in you; then the same words that apply to Jesus apply to you."

So, you see, My child, Satan HAS NOTHING IN YOU!

Satan has no claim on you.
Satan has nothing in common with you.
There is nothing in you that belongs to Satan.
Satan has no power over you. Selah!

Selah means ponder, and ponder is what I did. The following thoughts are what my pondering produced: If Jesus, when facing His crucifixion, says He will *not talk much* with those around him, then...

> *I purpose to imitate Him. I may stumble and fall at times, but by His strength, I will shut up, look up, get up, and try again to **not talk much**.

*I purpose to keep all griping, complaining, and negative words from my lips, and to speak only those things which will edify others and glorify God.

*I purpose to not allow others to speak the lies of the enemy in my presence and to surround myself with like-minded believers who will speak the truths of God's promises to me. If I am unable to find those who will so speak, then I, like David in I Sam. 30:6, will encourage and strengthen myself in the Lord my God.

*I purpose to pray in the spirit, sing and listen to praise music, take heed to Christian teachings, pastors' sermons, YouTube videos, TV programs, and Christian books.

*But, above all, as long as my strength remains, I will READ and FEED on the WORD of GOD because His words are life to me when I find them. They are healing and health to all my flesh, and I know that *my* death and *my* life lie in the power of *my* tongue... and I CHOOSE LIFE! (Prov.4:22; Prov. 18:21; Deut. 30:19)

So, if you hear these four little words DID GOD REALLY SAY? when going through any trial or temptation, remember this: You really can...***not talk much***. A simple, one-syllable word spoken *loud and clear* will suffice. That word is **YES!**

Dine in or Drive-thru?

In Psalm 23 God tells me that He prepares a table *before* me in the presence of my enemies. I realized one day that, for years, I have incorrectly quoted that verse by saying, "God prepares a table *for* me...," always assuming, of course, that it was *for* me. Which, by the way, I believe is true. It is *for* me.

But as I pondered this one little word *before*, I was suddenly struck with this thought: God prepares the table *before* me (in front of me), but I have to decide whether or not I am going to sit down and eat with Him in the *very presence* of my enemies.

Following is the script of the word-picture scenario, starring God and me, that began to play in my mind:

Me: There You are, God, preparing a table full of bountiful, sumptuous food just for me, and You are doing it right in the *very presence* of Satan and his demonic hoard. There it is. Right before my very eyes. Calling. Tempting. Waiting. Waiting for me to decide whether or not to sit down and partake of all the wonderful food You are offering me.

God: Yes, I know. What are you waiting for?

Me: What am I waiting for You ask? Well, God, You know my acceptance of your invitation is not all that 'cut and dried'. Don't You see the enemy all around? They are closing in on me. You know

I've been in the valley of the Shadow of Death. I've been fighting these demons with everything within me for a long time. I can't let down now. What will happen if I stop in the middle of the battle to feast at the table that's 'smack dab' in the middle of the enemy's camp? I might lose all the ground I've gained.

God: Aren't you getting tired in this battle?

Me: Yes, of course I am. I'm so tired and weary of fighting. You just don't know.

God: (smiling, says softly) Oh, I think perhaps I do know. Wouldn't you like a little respite?

Me: Yes, oh yes! It sounds wonderful to be able to stop and rest. To sit long and savor the bountiful spread You have so lovingly pre-pared for me. Just to sit in Your presence and breathe in Your love and peace would be so wonderful.

God: So, why don't you?

Me: Well, Lord, what would happen to my armored tank if I stepped out of it and just left it by the roadside? Would it be there when I returned? What if the enemy destroyed it? What would I do then? What would happen to my weapons of war if I laid them aside for a time of dining and communing leisurely with You? Would I be able to put them back on quickly enough to fight if the enemy attacked or would all my weapons be destroyed by my foe?

Perhaps it would be better if I just drove my tank through the drive-thru. I could grab a fistful of fast food and feast on it in a frenzy as I rush madly on to the next phase of **my** war. That way I wouldn't lose the momentum I have built up, and I could continue on with

my battle plan as **I** head back down to the valley of the Shadow of Death with **my** armored tank, **my** weapons, and **my** own strength.

So, you see, the decision is not as simple as one might think. **I** have much to ponder before **I** make my choice. Should **I** stop and eat at Your table or should **I** keep going and eat on the run?

There, Lord, You have it. That's **my** dilemma, **my** quandary. In the midst of **my** battle, do **I** *DINE IN or DRIVE-THRU?* It is a question that only **I** can answer.

God: **I** know, My Child. **I** know. **I**'ll just be here waiting for **you** to make…**your** decision.

Do You Think God Made a Mistake on This One?

I have been pondering the ~~Supreme, supreme, high~~…the Court's decision concerning the legalization of homosexual marriage. All I feel is a deep sadness.

Why do some classify those of us who are against this ruling as 'haters'? I am against the legalization of homosexual marriage, and yet I don't hate homosexuals. I am personally acquainted with six homosexuals whom I consider friends. They are all kind, personable, friendly, sensitive, caring, loving people. I value their friendship. I have positive, good, warmhearted feelings toward them and truly enjoy their company. I don't hate or fear them. I'm not a homophobe. I do not irrationally, unfairly, or intolerantly dislike them. I am not a bigot.

I am a Christian, a follower of Jesus. In my own personal study of the word of God, I try, to the best of my ability, to understand the ways God would have me to live. I then, again to the best of my ability, try to walk out those ways. Do I always succeed? Absolutely not! That's why I became a Christian. I needed Jesus to 'clean me up' and then help me learn to be who He wants me to be (which I confess takes continual 'cleaning up.')

I cannot convince you that God is real or that His word is true. It's your choice whether or not you believe, but I believe He is real, and I believe what He says is true, and God says:

Do not be deceived or misled, the
> *Liars*
> *Lewd*
> *Impure*
> *Thieves*
> *Fearful*
> *Those who participate in homosexuality*
> *Immoral*
> *Idolaters*
> *Adulterers*
> *Cheaters*
> *Murderers*
> *Swindlers*
> *Drunkards*
> *Slanderers*
> *Extortionists*
> *Unbelieving*
> *Abominable*
> *Foul-mouthed Revilers*
> *and Practicers of magic arts*

will not inherit or have any share in the kingdom of God.

This pretty much covers every living, breathing human being on the earth, don't you think?

Because I believe the Bible, I believe all of these are sins. **ALL** of them! And we are all guilty of some of them. Accepting God's method of getting rid of them is to accept what His Son did for us on the cross.

I praise God that after giving us this list of sins, He then shows His great mercy, grace, and love for us when He says this is the way we were *before* we were sanctified and justified by Jesus. But now we have been forgiven and can walk in newness of life. In Christ we have become a new creation and by the power of His Holy Spirit can have victory over these former sins. Thank You, Jesus!

My question, as a Christian who whole-heartedly believes God means what He says in the Bible, is this: How can man take homosexuality from the list of sins in God's Word and say that it is no longer a sin? How can the 'created' say to the 'Creator' that what He calls a sin is no longer a sin simply because we want it to not be a sin? How can we think God got that one sin in the list wrong? How can we say, "I think You made a mistake on this one, God."?

If this is what a nation chooses to believe it can do, what is to keep that nation from making the same proclamation about any or all of the aforementioned sins? What is to stop that nation from 'progressing backward' to the time when God says: *Every man did what was right in his own eyes?* If abominations and immorality were to, one day, be removed from this list of sins, would we then conclude that things like pedophilia, human trafficking (slavery) and murder would no longer be wrong? Would we then be identifying ourselves not only as Christian homosexuals, but as Christian pedophiles, Christian liars, Christian slave owners, Christian murderers, etc.?

This is why when I see our nation rejecting God's laws and drawing closer to a time when *man is (again) doing what is right in his own eyes*; my heart becomes overwhelmed with sadness. NOT hatred, but sadness.

If we Christians really hated others, we wouldn't care what they did. We wouldn't care if they didn't *inherit or have any share in the kingdom of God.* But we do care because God cared for us. We do love because God loved us. We know what we once were. We know what Jesus saved us from. We know how He changed our lives. We know who we are and Whose we are; and we just want to pass on to others the peace, the joy, the forgiveness, the freedom, and the love that we have received from God.

So, you see, as a Christian, I'm not trying to push my agenda on everyone. I'm trying to push everyone, who doesn't know how much God loves them, into His arms.

Don't Ever Forget How Much I Love You

To my wonderful mom on your special day
Across the miles this comes your way
To remind you today and all year through
Don't ever forget how much I love you.

Every day and night I thank the Lord above
For giving me a mother so full of love,
So kind and understanding with patience so true.
Don't ever forget how much I love you.

Though it's not said as often as it should be:
Thank you for the love and support you give me,
For all that you've done and all you still do,
Don't ever forget how much I love you.

I really do wish that I could be there
To give you a hug to show how I care.
You're the BEST mother and grandmother too.
Don't ever forget how much I love you.

I hope it is clear that you I do miss
And for you I am saving a Mother's Day kiss.
So, until next year, I hope and I pray
That this will be your BEST Mother's Day!

AND DON'T EVER FORGET HOW MUCH I LOVE YOU!!!

Love, Kevin

This was written by my son, Kevin Kerns, who could not make it home for Mother's Day one year. It is one of my priceless treasures, and blesses me every time I read it.

Finding Glory in My Night

few weeks ago, I was reading John 13:30-32 when God whispered these familiar words to my soul and made them new.

The setting is the last supper, and Judas, *having received the bread, went out immediately: and it was night. When he was gone out, Jesus spoke: Now is the Son of man glorified, and God is glorified in Him…*

Three words stood out as I read: **NIGHT! SPOKE! NOW!**

Night: All this took place at *night*, and it was a hard *night* for Jesus. *Night* is a time when things in my life are not looking so good.
Spoke: Jesus *spoke* the word of God in His *night*. I, too, need to *speak* the word of God in my *night*.
Now: *Now*, in the *night* of His life, Jesus was glorified. *Now*, in the *night* of my life, I can see Jesus glorified in me.

I can expect to see Jesus glorify Himself inside me. In my soul, the very God of gods will demonstrate the power I need to combat the enemy. In my flesh, I (and all those around me, including my enemy) will see Him glorified and working in my life as His mighty strength enables me to walk in victory. Within me, the glory of God can shine forth as I see the *night* approaching. He has *spoken* to me, through these words, telling me He will glorify Himself through me and in me *now*. He will not delay

He is encouraging me to speak forth His words in my difficult circumstances, to not lose hope, and to look expectantly for Him to show Himself mighty in me without delay.

Therefore, I purpose to not let my heart become distressed or agitated or fearful when I see my 'Judas' taking the bread and going out, thus ushering in my **night.**

I purpose to believe and **speak** God's word, trusting in Him and His power to do what He says He will do.

I purpose to see Him glorified in the **now** of my life as I go forth like Jesus to face my *night.*

Will you join me?

Footprints

I saw him once, on his *birth* day
For only a moment of time.
My heart and arms ached to reach out
And hold this son of mine.

We'd waited for him with such hope in our hearts,
Such plans, such dreams, such joy;
And now it seemed we'd never know
This precious little boy.

The cry of my heart could only be heard
By my Father up above.
The ache in my arms could only be healed
By His unfathomable love.

And then my Father, with a gentle voice,
Said, "Look up. I'm on the throne.
Your son is here; he's safe with Me,
Just waiting 'til you get Home."

So, though he'll be gone from us for awhile
And our hearts must bear the pain,
Someday our tears will be no more
And we'll be together again.

Some think the record of his birth
Are tiny footprints on a chart;
But our son, Peter, left much more…
He left footprints on our hearts!

*I wrote this for my daughter, Kim, and her husband, Pete,
in memory of their firstborn son, Peter Gerrard Baer II*

From Babies to Barbies... and Back

From *Babies to Barbies*, my mind rang out.
I looked up from my work and smiled.
My sewing lay limp, and my mind went back
As I thought of my youngest child.

I remembered a baby so tiny and sweet
As I held her close to my heart.
I thought of her, my blessing from God,
And I felt my memories start.

Those precious moments, months, and years
Didn't seem so very long ago.
I closed my eyes and could almost hear
Her high-pitched voice say, "SO!"

I saw blond hair flying as she skipped off to school,
Books banging against skinny legs.
I heard her voice at breakfast calling,
"Mother, 'smish' up my eggs."

I could see her sitting on the living room floor
For hours and hours on end,
Arranging furniture, making a home
Just right for 'Barbie and Ken.'

Small arms flapping and thighs being slapped
As she practiced cheers and routines,
Experiments with make-up, learning to drive,
A budding young lady in jeans.

Of the memories I'd gathered throughout the years,
One I remembered the most
Was the cry that came forth from those rose petal lips
When appalled or disgusted, "OH GROSS!"

The years have gone, the time has passed quickly,
And now she is all grown.
My little girl has put her *Barbies* away...
She's having a baby of her own.

This was written after learning I was going to become a 'Nana' for the very first time.

God's Grace and Prayer

itting on my porch swing, during one of her visits, I asked my friend, Mary Ann, how she kept such a peaceful, gentle spirit, day in and day out, as she dealt with the resurfacing effects of her husband's lifetime battle with polio. "How do you do it? How do you stay so joyful? What are some of the practical things you do?" I queried.

"Well," she answered, "probably the most helpful advice I ever received was from a former polio-battler. She told me to *do whatever you can while you can and live in the moment.* That piece of advice went straight to my heart, and for the last twenty years or so, we have been practicing walking out that advice. We keep busy doing the things we most like to do."

She then told me that learning to let go of worry about the future was a huge hurdle for her in the quest for peace. "That *letting go,*" she said quietly, "came about by prayer."

My dear friend is one of the most peaceful, joyful, gentle, humble women I have ever known. She would never describe herself in these words, but trust me, they fit her like a glove...a dainty, white, tea-party-ladylike glove. Every word of her testimony describing how she walks out each day in actual peace, joy, and gentleness in the Lord is always undergirded with this phrase: *It's by God's grace and prayer.* Ever so gently, not preachy or self-exalting, those simple words giving glory to the Lord always seem to slip gracefully into our conversation.

"My serenity is proportional to my expectations," she said. "Acceptance is the answer to all my problems. We can't do everything that everyone else does, so when I stopped worrying about fitting into everyone else's plans and started focusing on plans for us, I found peace. When I stopped being embarrassed about our situation and limitations and began to concentrate on what we *could* and *wanted* to do, I began to find contentment and freedom."

Her next words barreled into my heart like a quarterback crashing through the defensive line for a winning touchdown: *The understanding and acceptance of friends is so important.*

My soul fell to its knees in silence as I heard the Holy Spirit instantly speak the following words, "*The understanding and acceptance of friends are not just simply important,*" He said. "*In My kingdom, they are a must!*"

I knew, at that very moment, God had handed to me a mandate and a precious tool to use in helping those facing the often misunderstood, lonely, energy-and-soul-sucking ministry of a caregiver. One of the most important factors in a caretaker's ability to find peace, joy, contentment, and strength as he or she walks through the God-offered opportunity to care for a loved one in a time of deep need is ME…and YOU.

We *must* strive diligently to understand what those precious, caregiving saints are encountering as they walk out their call from God at this time in their lives.

We *must* try to comprehend, to the best of our ability, the limitations they are facing and the burdens they are bearing.

We *must* learn to accept them at all times and in all conditions with understanding, patience, joy, and unconditional love.

And how are we to do this? Quiet-spoken words tumble gently into my ear: *By God's grace and prayer.*

Thank you, Mary Ann, for your godly wisdom. I will try, *by God's grace and prayer*, to follow your example. And although you are much younger than I am, I want to be just like you...when I grow up.

God's Jolly Green Giant

While pondering a teaching on exercising our spiritual gifts, this question paraded unexpectedly through my mind, "Are you a jolly green giant?"

"Huh?" I exclaimed. "A jolly green giant?"

The question turned around abruptly and marched back boldly. "Yes," it repeated. "Are you a jolly green giant...in the kingdom of God.?"

"Well, uh, just exactly what do you mean by that?"

Holy Spirit then began to speak. I began to listen.

ARE YOU JOLLY?

*Are you a walking advertisement for the joy of the Lord?

*Do you look as if you've been anointed with the oil of gladness as Jesus was?

*Being joyful can bring confusion to any darkness that is trying to rule over you and others in your life because joy brings light wherever it is released, and darkness can't overtake light. That's a rule... God's rule.

*The devil doesn't expect joy from you when you are going through a battle. He doesn't know how to fight joy.

*Joy is your strength. It's the enemy's weakness. So be a releaser of God's joy.

It is possible, you know. You can be JOLLY! (John 15:11)

"Well then," I answered. "I think I will be **JOLLY**."

ARE YOU GREEN?

*Are you like the evergreen tree, always growing, alive, exuding the fresh sweet fragrance of the Holy Spirit?

*Are you still as excited about your 'love-relationship' with Jesus as you were the first time you met Him?

*Or has your association with His love letters to you become so routine and blah that your soul longs to 'taste them again for the very first time' as the cornflakes cereal ad from long ago proclaimed?

*Are you still like a little child, or in cowboy language, are you still a *green*horn when you hear a new word from the Lord?

*Are you ever-learning? Eager to learn? Thrilled and energized when the word becomes life to you?

*Are you bold and courageous when spreading the Good News about Jesus?

*Is your spirit teachable or have you heard it all...know it all?

*Are you flexible, accepting of others' ways when they don't agree with your ways?

*Would you be described as *old and set in your ways* or *childlike and young at heart?*

It is achievable. You can be GREEN, you know." (Psalm 92:13,14)

"Well, then," I answered. "I think I will be **GREEN.**"

ARE YOU A GIANT?

*Are you aware of your spiritual authority, your power over the enemy?

*Do you comprehend the overpowering, unconditional, awesome love of your Father for you?

*Have you taken advantage of your access to God's endless reserves of grace, faith, hope, and power?

*Do you even realize the vastness of the infinite resources you have to enable you to meet every need in your life and the lives of others?

*Are you conscious of the very presence of God Himself living in you?

*Do you grasp the availability of the anointing you carry within yourself that equips you to bring all those you meet into a life-changing encounter with the God of the universe?

*Do you understand that Jesus has made it possible, by His death on the cross, to allow His anointing to flow out through you to others?

*Do you ever cry out for a greater anointing to pour forth from your life that you might break the yokes of bondage that hold your loved ones and neighbors captive?

*Do you covet the spiritual gifts so you can impart the presence of God to all who hunger and thirst?

It is doable. You can be a GIANT, you know. (Philippians 4:13)

"Well then," I declared. "I think I will be a **GIANT.**"

"Actually," Holy Spirit whispered in my ear, "I can help you be all three."

"Oh, Wow!" I shouted. "Then that's what I think I will be!

I think I will be a **JOLLY GREEN GIANT**…with Your help, Lord."

God's Little Helper

If you had only known what this saying means, you would not have condemned the guiltless: I desire mercy rather than sacrifice. I desire a readiness to help, a readiness to spare, a readiness to forgive. I desire this rather than sacrificial victims. Matthew 12:7

Whew, Lord, I'm pretty tired. I have had a really busy day. It's not easy helping You do Your work, You know. All that judging wears a body out! Oh, I'm not complaining, mind You. I like helping You. In fact, I think I have just about got this judging business down pat. I'm getting rather good at it if I do say so myself.

I know all about that business of not judging others, but it is not as if they're not guilty; and, after all, I am helping You. I am simply judging whether or not they are following Your rules. Well, OK, I admit that sometimes I judge whether or not they're following the rules the way I think they should be following them. But, after all, I have been a Christian for a *really looong* time; and I think I, of all people, should know what the rules are by now, don't You?

I figure I'm saving you quite a bit of work. I'm binding them up and placing them on the altar for You. I guess one could say I've got them *signed, sealed, and delivered.*

I have signed their confession for them.
I have sealed my mind and believe my judgments line right up with Yours.

I've delivered them up to You to take care of.

I guess You could look at them as my daily sacrifice. You know, sort of like a part of my *works* program.

I've done my best, Lord. I've judged how their *works* have not measured up to Your standards (and my standards too, of course.) I know how much You desire holiness and good works, so I'm glad to be doing my part in helping You get rid of their unholiness. No need to thank me, no need at all. I'm proud to be of service. It's all in a day's work, and it looks as if my work is just about finished for today.

Uh, wait just one second, God. I want to step back away from the altar. I don't want to be standing too close. You know, just in case one of those sparks might...well, I don't want to be mistaken for one of my *sacrificial victims*.

OK. Go ahead, God. It's all clear now. Send down Your fire!

God's Story About Me

God says His eyes saw me before I was even formed, and in His book all the days of my life were written before they ever took shape. (Psalm 139:16.)

Wow! God has written a story in His Book all about me! Oh God, I do so want it to be a good story. A story that others love to read. I don't want it to be boring, but I doubt You could write anything boring.

Father, make my story plain. Make it easy for those who are reading it to understand. Make it deep though, not full of fluff. Make it light and cheery in certain parts so that those who are hurting will be lifted up and encouraged. Make it rich and strong so those who are hungry for You will be fed. Make it real. Make it transparent. And would You make it funny in some parts?

Most of all, Lord, don't make me the main character. I want You to be the Star, the Hero, of my story. Let all my adventures and every chapter and page center around You. But, if You don't mind, I'd like to be the second most important star in it...except maybe not in the chapter about pride. Could You just leave me out of that chapter? No, I suppose that wouldn't be right, would it? Well, maybe You could make that chapter short.

I hope I appear brave and wise and kind and loving and humble like Jesus; and I want to ride off at the end of my story on a mighty warhorse with my Prince Jesus to live happily ever after. One more thing, Father. If I'm not being too presumptuous, could You make it be on the best-seller list, at least for a day or two?

Lastly, Abba, when I stand before You at the end of my life holding my book in my hands, would You let it be well-worn from being read and used by others? And could the final words of the last chapter be Yours saying, "Well done, good and faithful servant."?

Growing Mold or Growing Bold?

*L*ately I have been pondering a lot about growing old. Perhaps it's because I am, but then everyone is, aren't they? Somehow, when *one* has passed the 70-year mark, *one* seems to notice it much more, especially if I happen to be that *one*.

I'm not sure I know just how to go about being old. How do people know how to grow old anyway? It seems to me that everyone wants to live a long time, but no one wants to be old. I don't know about you, but since I can't avoid this universal phenomenon, I have decided I want to learn *how* to be old. I want to know *how* to approach this experience with anticipation and *boldness*. I want to explore just how I can participate in it with wisdom, joy, and contentment.

I refuse to simply *grow old and mold*. I have made my children 'pinkie-swear' that if they ever detect that *old people smell* hovering around me, they will lovingly and gently say to me, "Hey Mom, we bought you some new perfume. Want to try it?"

We have all heard that sentimental saying: *Grow old with me...the best is yet to come.* Well, I believe, with all my heart, that God intends for us to grow old with grace and gladness, and 'by cracky' I'm going to do it if it kills me. I have announced to all my friends that I will be dragging them right along with me in this quest because no matter how old they are now, one day they're going to find them-selves spending more time in the geriatric aisle of the pharmacy than anywhere else, and they can *Depend*(s) on that.

So, for starters to help us get a view of what God intends for old age to look like, we need to make friends with *older* Christian saints. (Although at my age, I may have to look a little harder to find those I can classify as *older.*) We need to find precious men and women of God who have *been there, done that, and gotten the T-shirt.* Saints who have accumulated decades of God-years of experience... years filled with love and loss, laughter and sorrow, success and failure, joy and heartache, in other words, years filled with walking with Jesus in ordinary, every-day living. We need to ask (no, we need to beg) them to share those glorious, God-filled, lesson-loaded years with us.

We need to sit humbly at their feet and soak in the FAITH, the LOVE, the TRUST, and the HOPE that has brought them to where they are at this time in their lives. We need to position our hearts to listen as they share about how their Father God has led them and made them who they are today in Jesus Christ: mighty men and women of prayer, strong moral character, spiritual strength, godly wisdom, and hope.

To prepare our souls to be nourished and refreshed, we must have a desire, a thirst, to listen, learn, laugh, and cry with God's very own precious, much loved, refreshingly real, mighty warriors of faith.

So, if you, like me, plan on growing old, minus the mold, let's pray God will help us find some precious older saints who can teach us how to be bold as we face this new adventure called *growing old.*

Happy 70th Birthday, Mom!!!

I am blessed with the greatest mom that a girl could ever hope to have! She is such an amazing woman and the biggest inspiration to me. Today my mom is celebrating her 70th birthday!

Seventy will NEVER again seem old to me. I think that my mother has more energy than I do! She is ALWAYS busy: taking care of her home and hubby; caring for my 92 year old grandma who lives with her; encouraging a friend or acquaintance with visits, phone calls or cards; spending time reading her Bible, praying and writing in her journal, planning the Women's Gatherings at church, rearranging her furniture (monthly, it seems!)…the list goes on and on!

Growing up with my mom was so much fun! I remember that all of my friends wished that they had MY mom! They thought she was SO COOL!! Even at that young age, I knew that my mom was a gift! Some of my most vivid memories of my childhood home are of my mom laughing and singing. She always had her church hymnal propped up on the window sill above the kitchen sink. And lots of Bill Gaither on the record player! She even taught herself to play the ukulele! (Yeah, it was a little scary…lol)

My mom has had her share of heartaches and hard times. Through her trials, she has shown me what real faith looks like. She has shown me that life doesn't have to be perfect for us to have peace and joy. When my 'young self' looks back and remembers laughter and singing, my 'grown-up self' knows that she was a newly single mom of three kids, barely getting by.

And this little girl was always watching her and wanting to be like her. She has been such a wonderful example of a faithful servant of God. I hope someday that I can 'live' my faith the way she does. I have never known a more caring and giving woman. She is always ready to help someone with an encouraging word, a card, or a meal. She is truly His hands and feet, busy doing His work.

My mom loves to have her family all together. Our family is much larger these days, so it makes for a houseful! As stressful as that can be, Mom lovingly plans meals and decorates her home to make our holidays together extra special. She has always wanted a "Walton table", a big, LONG table that the whole family can sit around together! (Pass the salt, John Boy! Thanks, Jim Bob!) The more, the merrier!

My brother, sister, and I are so blessed because our mom has shown us unconditional love. What a gift to know that your mom loves you fiercely, prays for you constantly, and looks forward eagerly to our next visit or conversation. (Yes, we are spoiled, too!!!)

Mom, I hope that you have an AMAZING, relaxing birthday. Know that you are loved!

Love, Kim

Written by my daughter, Kim Baer, on March 9, 2011. (Would you believe I keep this in my bedside table and read it sometimes when I need a 'word hug' from God?)

Ho-Ho-Ho's from Heaven

A few years ago, a friend and I had a lively debate about whether or not God laughs. I said He did. My friend said He did not. I went to the Bible to try to prove my point. In my searching of the word laugh, when applied to God, I could only find that He laughs at His enemies and calamities. Although technically I won the debate, it was not the kind of laughter I had had in mind. I was looking for the word laughter to be connected to a happy laughter coming from Him.

I thought of what our pastor says at the end of each service as he quotes Numbers 6:25.
The Lord make His face shine upon you.... Then I looked at Psalm 67:1. *...cause His face to shine upon us.* Psalms 31:16 and 119:135 say: *Make Your face shine upon Your servant....* My conclusion was and is that when God makes His face shine on me, He is smiling; and if He can smile, He can laugh. It has been said that the Bible may not actually say God laughs, but He sure made us so that we can, and I totally agree.

We know the Bible says that *Jesus wept* and that He is called a *man of sorrows*, but the Bible also says that He was *anointed with the oil of joy above His fellows*. Joy makes one laugh, so Jesus must have laughed. Words make us laugh...Jesus is the Word...so Jesus must make us laugh.

I had asked God for a 'Life verse' many years ago, and He gave me Genesis 21:6: *God has made me to laugh so that all who hear will laugh with me.* Since that time, my prayer has been that I would continue throughout my life to be a walking testimony of my 'Life verse.' I thank God daily for His wonderful gift to me, my sense of humor. (I am also thankful He gifted someone with the idea to invent Depends.)

Listen to the greetings we give to one another at Christmas time: *Merry* Christmas, *Happy* Holidays, *Joy* to the World, *Glad* Tidings. They all have gladness and laughter embedded in them, and we bless and encourage one another with these words. I believe that even though the world is filled with sorrow, pain, and trials, the Lord encourages us to live lives filled with joy and laughter. I also believe if it weren't possible, He would not have asked us to do it.

I would like to encourage you this Christmas season and all seasons, to make an effort to practice joy and laughter, so I have put together a few tips to help you get started. Most of these tips center around your refrigerator because that's where we spend most of our time, at least during the holidays. So here we go:

*Buy a small chalkboard, glue magnets to the back, put it on the 'fridge, and write words on it that make you chuckle.

*Paint an old metal sign, pie pan, cake plate, etc., with chalkboard paint, attach magnets, hang on 'fridge, write, and laugh.

*Buy small magnets, write jokes on paper, cut out pictures, cartoons, etc. that make you smile and stick them on the 'fridge.'

*Use clear plastic picture frames to insert your funnies in. They are already magnetized.

*Use sticky notes (if you don't suffer from OCD) and plaster them anywhere.

*Need funny stuff to write? Look on Facebook, Google, Pinterest, or watch your family.

*Then LAUGH...GOD DOES!

How Do You Do?

As she entered the church on her first day,
Not one person spoke as they passed her way.
An usher greeted her, "*How do you do?*"
Then turned away to greet someone he knew.

She stood there alone and wondered why
Some people smiled, but they all passed her by.
"I'm new," she said to a lady who passed.
"*How do you do?* You can come to my class."

She was led to the class with no chit-chat,
Just one "*How do you do?*" and that was that.
The woman's welcome had come to an end
As she left to go sit with her best friend.

The teacher approached with a friendly look,
"*How do you do?* Sign our visitors' book."
Then he proceeded to greet the others:
All the 'regular' sisters and brothers.

One person nodded, and after a while,
She was acknowledged with a wave and a smile.
After class one stopped, said, "*How do you do?*"
But soon hurried off with, "Was nice to meet you."

She followed the crowd and soon was seated.
"*How do you do?*" was how she was greeted.
Then the pastor said as they all sat down,
"Welcome to the friendliest church in town."

This statement was met with clapping and shouts,
Visitors acknowledged; packets passed out.
Folks smiled and waved at all those who were new.
Some shook her hand, saying, "*How do you do?*"

The church overflowed with worship and praise,
And people were blessed in so many ways.
But as she left, just two people did speak.
One: "*How do you do?*" One: "Come back next week."

Her visit to church had come to an end,
But she hadn't made even one new friend.
If Jesus were watching and judging you,
When visitors visit…*How do you do?*

I Need You

Have you ever felt battle-weary, lonely, and judged? If so, would you stretch your creative imaginations with me as I try to express what God spoke to me, personally, through Psalm 55:16-18?

Psalm 55:16-18 (KJV)
16) As for me, I will call upon God; and the Lord shall save me.
17) Evening, and morning, and at noon will I pray, and cry aloud:
and He shall hear my voice.
18) He has delivered my soul in peace from the battle that was against
me: for there were
*many with me.

Verse 18 cries out **Victory!** Ah yes, but only the Lord and I know what has actually transpired in that period between verses 17 and 18… that period between turmoil and tranquility.

You may see my scars and hear my victory cry, but only God and I have felt the cost.

Only my Father and I know of the struggles I must overcome *daily* to continue to walk in victory.

Will you not judge me too harshly when my scars cause me to limp in areas where you can run? Will you not label me when my victory cry at times becomes a mere whimper because I am flesh… and sometimes weak?

Will you look at me, not through your eyes, but God's?

Will you hold out your hand to me? Will you love me unconditionally whether I am crying aloud in the thick of battle, rejoicing in soul peace from the victory, or standing wearily somewhere in between verses 17 and 18?

Will you be one of the *many with me*?

I need you…for Victory.

Bear one another's burdens and so fulfill the law of Christ. Galatians 6:2

* I realize the words *many with me* is being referred to by the psalmist in a different light than what I saw at the time God was using these verses to minister to me, but He used those words in the way I have written about them to touch my soul.

If Only

arly one morning I heard these words, *"You are in Christ. Christ is perfect, and He is seated in heaven with God. Therefore, if you are in Christ, then you are seated with God and are already perfect in heaven."*

"Humm," I thought, "I believe that. So, what's going on with me down here on earth? I'm in Christ, but I don't seem to be very perfect."

The next words, marching through my brain, caught my attention. *"Here on earth you are in the process of becoming who you already are."*

"Huh?"

I was still pondering these words as I began reading my scripture for the day:

Behold, a virgin shall be with child and shall bring forth a Son. (Matthew 1:23)

When I saw this familiar Christmas scripture, I wondered what God was going to say to me personally through these words. I was fairly certain it wasn't simply going to be *Merry Christmas*...and I was right.

He began with this question: *"When you received the good news of what Jesus had done for you on the cross and were born again, do you know what actually took place?"* Before I could even begin to think of an answer, He continued. *"You became a new creation, a brand-new woman. You became a virgin, spiritually speaking. I took you for My bride. I then planted within you My very own Seed. What was conceived in you was the Holy Spirit of My Son. My declaration over you was that you would bring forth My Son, and His name would be Jesus."*

Whoa! These were words that were going to take a while to digest. So, I pondered the following four points:

*When I was born again, I became the virgin bride of Christ.

*God planted into my spirit the very Seed of His Son, Jesus, in the form of the His Holy Spirit.

*I am now *with Child*, spiritually speaking, as I carry Jesus inside of me.

*God has proclaimed that *I shall bring forth THE SON.*

My brain and heart went into overload mode! Here we are on earth, and we have Jesus, God's Son, living in us. We are, in the spirit, actually in the process of bringing Him forth in our lives for all the world to see!

I continued reading about Joseph purposing to quietly put Mary away until he heard the words from the angel...*for that which is conceived in her is of the Holy Spirit.* He then did a complete about-face. He had seen Mary's sin or what, in his eyes, appeared to be sin, and he wanted her out of his life. But when God spoke to him, he listened and began to see Mary's so-called sin from God's perspective.

Many times, when we see the *perceived* sins of others, we are quick to condemn and want to 'put them away'…out of our lives. Sadly, unlike Joseph, we often don't want to *quietly* 'put them away.' We want to expose their *assumed* sin through gossip, backbiting or 'sharing with others so they can pray about it.'

We look at the imperfect lives of our brothers and sisters in Christ and make our judgments, forgetting that here on earth they are carrying the very Son of God within them. We need to remember (however imperfectly it may seem in our estimation) they are trying, to the best of their ability, to *bring forth the Son of God* in their lives. We, unlike Joseph, often have our ears closed to the voice of God because we view them, not from God's perspective, but from the world's.

Oh, Lord,

If only we could be more like Joseph.

If only we could hear Your voice when we so quickly judge and condemn the actions of others.

If only we could see them as You see them.

If only we could keep them in our lives and not want to 'put them away' either physically or emotionally.

If only we could hold them close to our hearts and protect them from the condemnation.

If only we could remember that they are in the process of becoming who they *already are in heaven*.

*If only we could be like Joseph and stand by them and love them as they labor to *bring forth the Son into the world.*

Oh, Lord, *IF ONLY...*

In a Storm?
Cheer Up! Huh?

Be of good cheer; it is I, be not afraid. (Matthew 14:27)

I find it interesting that the first word Jesus said to the disciples when they were struggling for their lives in the middle of a terrifying storm was *be*. He did not tell them to *do*. He told them to *be*. *Be* means to become. *Do* means to perform. I also think it astonishing that He was instructing them, in the midst of their fear, to become cheerful (full of cheer.)

Excuse me, Jesus. No offense intended, but I have been filled with real fear before. We are talking about heart-pounding, heat-pouring-through-my-whole-body, breath-stopping, hands-shaking fear. I'm pretty certain the first words I would want to hear would not be, "Cheer up." Why would You tell the disciples to become cheerful?

Another Bible translation says: *Take courage! I Am! Stop being afraid!* Now those words seem a little bit more plausible to my pea-sized brain. In my mind's eye I can see You, Jesus, sensing their fear as You watch them struggle. I can picture You lifting Your hands filled with a large dose of courage and shouting to them (I figure You had to shout because the wind was so loud, plus they were probably all screaming at each other in terror which would add to the noise level)…I can hear You shouting, "Here! Look in My hands.

I have courage for you! Take it! I AM GOD! I AM here to rescue you! You can relax now! You can stop being afraid! *Take this courage!"*

But the words that have grabbed my attention are these: *Be of good cheer.* It is something You are telling them to *be,* and it is something that seems impossible under the circumstances. Yet I believe You would not tell them to *be* something they couldn't.

So, Holy Spirit, what are You trying to show me here that is applicable to me and my life today? How can I, when fear strikes, *be* cheerful? That's just not something that comes natural to me. I'm figuring it's got to be one of those *super*-natural things You say can be done by me-if I just look, listen, and learn as You demonstrate the life-lesson You're teaching me. Oh Lord, help me to look. Help me to listen. Help me to learn. Help me to lean on You.

As I sat back in my porch swing pondering, I heard Father say, "My child, you are right in your understanding that I would never tell you to do something you are incapable of doing, something I understand would be impossible for you to do on your own. I said *be* and not *do* because there is no *do*ing. There is no work you have to perform in the midst of fear. The work, the *do*ing, has already been done by Me on the cross. Whatever it is you think you need to *do,* you don't.

I did all the performing, exerting, sweating, and striving that ever needs to be done. All of that is finished. I did all the *doing* (or work) so that I, in Spirit form, could come and live in you; therefore, enabling you to no longer have to perform, exert, sweat, strive, or work. You would simply have to *be. Be*-lieve that every word I say is true. It is all very simple really. I did all the *do* so you can just *be* all the *be,* and the way you can *be* all the *be* is to *be*-lieve Me when I say I have done all the *do.*

Trust Me when I say you can be filled with cheer (hope, courage, comfort, gladness, rejoicing) in any life-threatening, fear-filled situation. You can be of good cheer if you know Who I AM. I AM GOD. I AM all-powerful, all-knowing, all-able to handle every situation in your life. I have everything under control. I AM with you in every storm. Read Matthew 14:27 again. Notice where I AM. Do you see Me? Look at the words describing Me. IT IS I! Do you see me now? There I AM right in the middle of good cheer and fear.

There may be times when Satan will catch you off-guard, and you will start to be filled with fear, but remember, I AM there. I have everything under control. I AM stronger than any devil who, in the midst of your storm, is screaming, 'Be afraid! Be very afraid!' The more you spend time with Me, the more you will realize how very powerful I AM and how very much I love you. The more you realize My love for you, the more you will experience the fullness of cheer and the lack of fear inside you when you find yourself facing a hurricane-strength storm.

You have a choice, My beloved. You can go into your storm at the beginning, taking courage from Me and being of good cheer. Or you can wait and suffer in fear for a while, in the midst of it, before you take courage and become of good cheer.

My desire is for you **not** to wait until you are in the midst of a storm, or at the end of one to sense My presence. My desire is for you to know I AM with you at the beginning because I AM with you *always.* I AM in the beginning...the middle...and the end. *I will never leave you or forsake you.* Oh, how much easier it would be for you if you would choose me at the beginning.

IT IS I! *Be* of good cheer, b*e* not afraid.

It is Going to Be a Shiny New Year

One morning I awoke at 12:30 a.m. with two words exploding in my head: PSALM 67. It wasn't the actual words of Psalm 67 because I had no idea what they were. It was simply the two words: *PSALM 67*.

What happened next was, in itself, a small miracle. You see I play this little game when I awake in the middle of the night for one of my many trips to the bathroom. As I grope my way falteringly to my destination, I do one of three things: I keep both eyes tightly closed and flail my arms wildly in front of me so I won't crash into the walls, or I open one eye only slightly, or I squint through tiny slits in both eyes pretending they are not open. I do this to trick my body into thinking I am not really awake, so that when I get back in bed, I won't lie there trying to go back to sleep for the next two or three hours.

So, the miracle part is that I actually turned on the light and began to read PSALM 67. I was excitedly looking for some kind of lightning bolt to strike because the impression of those two words on my mind had been so strong when I awoke. I truly believed God had a message for me.

I must confess that I was glad when I realized it was a short Psalm, consisting of only seven verses, because I was extremely tired. (I know, I know, doesn't sound very spiritual, does it?) Anyway, I read it…all seven verses! It took me longer than one might think because twice in those seven verses it said to SELAH. So, I had to pause and calmly think about what I had read. (That's what SELAH means.) It's a little difficult at midnight to SELAH with joy when you're tired, and the bathroom tile is really cold on your bare feet. But I tried, honestly, I did.

I'm sorry to announce that as I read it, there were no lightning bolts, no bells, no flapping of angels' wings and no goose bumps. (Well, there were perhaps a few goose bumps because of the cold tile floor.) At first glance this Psalm seemed pretty 'cut and dried.' But I've learned over the many years I've been walking with the Lord that not one *'little'* word of His is ever 'cut and dried.' I have been blessed beyond measure so many times by just one of His *'little'* words, (i.e., the word BUT, as in "but God."). So, at 12:45 a.m., I decided to begin my journey through PSALM 67 (asking, seeking, reading, praying, SELAH-ing) to find the treasure God wanted to give me in His word. I began with verse 1: "God be merciful to us, and bless us; and **cause His face to shine upon us.** Selah."

Now, lest you think I am trying to impress you with my spirituality, I'd like to fast forward to the very next afternoon after my midnight encounter with this Psalm. For many years, every December, I have asked God to give me a word for the coming year to study and ponder, a special word to touch my life, encourage me, and cause me to grow in Him.

So, that afternoon as I was reading and thinking about PSALM 67, I suddenly became aware of the thoughts that were running through my head. "Oh, Lord," my thoughts thought, "I hope You're not going to give me *Psalm 67* for my word this year. It seems so… so unexciting, so matter of fact, so not full of deep secrets, so 'cut and dried.' Couldn't I maybe have one from Isaiah or Revelation or Nahum?"

Then quite unexpectedly, I personally experienced verse 1 of Psalm 67. I actually felt **God's face shine upon me** (which I translate to mean: He smiled at me)! **God shined at me! God, Himself, smiled at me!**

Do you know what I did when I realized what I had been thinking to God about His choice for my new year's word? I looked at my heavenly Father and **I shined right back at Him.** We shined at each other, and then we laughed out loud together.

I believe PSALM 67 is going to be an awesome word for me, and God and I are going to have a very **SHINY NEW YEAR!**

Jesus...With Skin On

Take care not to do your good deeds publicly in order to be seen by men...
(Matthew 6:1)

This verse is not telling us to sneak around and do all our good deeds where no one can see us. It is telling us to not make *being seen* doing those good deeds our motive.

How many times have you been touched and blessed when you have seen someone *putting on the apron, picking up the towel,* or *going the second mile* to perform some thoughtful, loving, or even unpleasant task? How many times have you been moved to imitate them?

I believe, if we as Christians analyzed this desire to be like them, we would realize it's not really the person we are wanting to emulate, but Jesus Himself. Because who we are actually seeing in those humble acts of selfless love is really Jesus...*with skin on.*

*It's Jesus *with skin on* smiling and chatting with that tired, sullen checkout girl.

*It's Jesus *with skin on* sending that small gift to someone just to brighten her day.

*It's Jesus *with skin on* giving the last piece of chocolate pie to someone else even though it's his favorite.

*It's Jesus *with skin on* holding the tiny baby during church to give that tired mother a small respite.

*It's Jesus *with skin on* sending that card just to say: Have a Nice Day.

*It's Jesus *with skin on* smiling and putting you first even when her own heart is heavy with disappointment.

*It's Jesus *with skin on* putting the shopping cart back in its corral on a cold day even when it's a loooong way from his parked car.

*It's Jesus *with skin on* REALLY listening after she has asked: How are you doing?

*It's Jesus *with skin on* visiting that elderly saint who has missed church for a couple of Sundays.

*It's Jesus *with skin on* letting someone with fewer items in her shopping cart go ahead of him in the checkout line.

*It's Jesus *with skin on* mopping the church basement floor, cleaning the bathrooms, mowing the lawn, and fixing things when no one is around to see.

*It's Jesus *with skin on* picking up that piece of clothing in the store and putting it back on the hanger even though she didn't knock it off.

*It's Jesus *with skin on* who greets you with a smile at the door every Sunday, rain or shine.

*It's Jesus *with skin on* rejoicing and dancing with you when you have just received wonderful news.

*It's Jesus *with skin on* with tears in her eyes when you are sharing the broken pieces of your heart with her.

*It's Jesus *with skin on* filling your soul with the Father's words of encouragement when your faith tank is running on empty.

*It's Jesus *with skin on* who makes you laugh so hard that coffee snorts out your nose.

*It's Jesus *with skin on* making a beeline for that visitor in church who no one else is talking to.

*It's Jesus *with skin on* who supplies the 'doughnuts' for the '5,000' Sunday after Sunday.

*It's Jesus *with skin on* loving you even at your 'unloveliest.'

*It's Jesus *with skin on* standing by you for the long haul after everyone else has gone.

*It's Jesus *with skin on* loving you enough to confront you in that 'little' or 'big' sin.

*It's Jesus *with skin on* who faithfully does those little things for you day after day without complaining.

*It's Jesus *with skin on* seeing your heart, the real you, and accepting you just the way you are.

How many times today have you missed an opportunity to let someone see Jesus...*with skin on?*

Just Keep Peddling

One summer morning I was sitting on my porch swing, drinking my first cup of chai, and pondering. I knew my Father loved me, but how could I get that head knowledge down into my heart? How could I practice daily *living loved*?

"Lord," I whispered, "I try. Every day. I really do. I try, I fail, I get discouraged. Then I start the whole process all over again. How can I overcome this roadblock in my spiritual progress? Sometimes I just feel like giving up. I feel like such a loser. How can You keep putting up with me? I don't think I measure up. I wonder if I ever will? I wonder if I will ever *learn* how to *live loved*?"

The next words quietly nudged their way into my thoughts, "Look across the street." As I did, I noticed a young mother in the church parking lot across from our home. She was in the process of trying to teach her small child to ride a bicycle minus the training wheels. As I watched that familiar run-along-beside-the-bike process (I had taught my own three children in the same painstakingly, back-bending way), Holy Spirit prompted me to go back in time and remember how it felt when I, myself, had learned to ride.

It was almost as if I were watching a movie. It was 1945. I was four years old. It was either pre-training-wheel days or we couldn't afford them, but I remember I didn't care. I just wanted to learn to ride that little, rusty, red bike! I could picture my daddy running along beside me holding onto the seat. I would be doing fine until

78

I'd get so engrossed in what I was doing that I'd forget to listen to his voice encouraging me. I would panic, thinking he was no longer there. And then, it would begin: the wobbling, the running into trees and mailboxes, the falling in the dirt, the crying, the feelings of discouragement, the feeling of being afraid to try again.

Instead of focusing on his encouraging words, I would begin hearing a taunting voice inside my head saying "You're never going to learn to do this on your own. You're going to be the only kid in the neighborhood whose daddy will be running along beside her on her bicycle. You'll never measure up. You can't do this. Why don't you just give up?"

But I also remember a still, small voice from somewhere deep down inside saying, "I am going to ride this bike. I want to feel the wind blowing through my hair. I want to ride fast! I am not going to give up!" Then I would say, "Daddy, can we try again?" He would smile and steady the bike while I climbed back up on the seat, and away we would go to repeat the whole process over and over.

Then, despite skinned knees, scraped elbows, dirt-covered clothes, tear-streaked cheeks (because some of those falls really hurt), despite all that, one miraculously glorious moment I found, much to my amazement, my hair was blowing in the wind, the handle bars weren't shaking, the front tire wasn't wobbling, the trees weren't standing in front of me to stop my forward progress (they were flying past me about a hundred miles an hour). I was flying in the wind!

Best of all, I could hear my daddy's voice behind me yelling at the top of his lungs, "I knew you could do it! Keep looking forward! Don't look back! Just keep peddling!"

After all these years, I can still hear his voice cheering, encouraging, urging me on. And do you want to know something? Never once did my daddy ever say to me, "You fell again. What's the matter with you? Why can't you do this? It's so easy. Look at all the other kids who can ride bikes! I can't believe you can't! You must be too stupid or immature or clumsy or scared to learn!"

He never said, "Stop crying! Don't be a big baby! I'm going to give you one more chance, and if you can't do it this time, that's it. I quit! I'm done trying to help you! You're impossible! You are such a loser! You will never measure up. I don't think you can do it. You might as well quit."

Never once did he give me bad advice. He was constantly instructing, encouraging, praising, and reassuring me that he would always be there right beside me to help me up, brush the dirt off, dry my tears with the big white handkerchief he always carried in his back pocket, straighten the bent fender, and help me get back on that bike again. The 'movie scene' faded.

"This," said the Holy Spirit, "is how you can *learn* to *live loved*. Lean on your Father as He leads, guides, encourages, comforts, and runs beside you. Just as your daddy taught you to put your right foot under the pedal to bring it up into just the right position so you would have more power as the pedal went down when you pushed off to start, your Father is teaching you to get in the right position to trust Him to help you to start to learn how to ride this new *bike* of *living loved* in your daily walk with Him. Trust is the right position you must get into to push off, and you can trust Him to help you do it."

"Your Father loves you, unconditionally, just the way you are! He doesn't care how many times in the past you have fallen off your *bike*, or how many times you fell off today, or how many times you are going to fall off in the future."

"If you listen, you will hear your Father's voice saying, 'You *can* do it! Get on that *bike*! You *can* conquer that fear of failing. That fear of not being good enough. That fear of falling short. That fear of *I can't*. If you listen closely, you will hear your Abba Daddy say, 'Get back on that *bike*. Trust Me. Together we will have you *flying in the wind*!'"

And suddenly I got it! No matter how many spills I took, no matter how many start-overs I did, no matter how many times I felt like a failure, all I had to do was look for my Father's Hand on the *bike* and listen for His Voice in my heart. If I would do this, I'd hear those familiar words calling to me, "I know you can do it! You can *learn* to *live loved*! Just keep peddling!"

As I prepared to leave my porch-swing pondering place, I smiled as I heard the young mother shouting at the top of her voice, "I know you can do it! You can learn to ride that bike!

Just keep peddling!"

Kingdom-Minded

s I was pondering Jesus' words: *Thy kingdom come. Thy will be done*, Holy Spirit began speaking quietly to my mind. "How many times have you prayed those words?" He asked.

"Probably hundreds," I answered proudly.

His next statement startled me. "Do you know that each time you have prayed those words, you have been praying them incorrectly?"

"Really?" I gulped.

"Yes, really," He gently chided. "You have been praying them as a request, a sort of *Lord, I hope it will happen someday plea;* an *I-want-it-to-happen-and-I'm-trying-my-best-to-do-my- part-to-make-it-come-to-pass-so-please-help-me* entreaty."

I was speechless.

"Would you like to know how your Father wants you to pray His words?"

"Oh, yes! Very much!" I cried.

Then Holy Spirit, my Teacher, my Guide, whispered to my heart, "Look and listen to the life-giving words of Jesus in your Spirit. *His words are Spirit, and they are Life.*"

As I began to meditate on these words, suddenly the eyes of my understanding were opened, and I saw, with Holy Spirit insight, the truth within Jesus' words: *Thy kingdom come. Thy will be done....*

"I see it, Father," I cried, "Your kingdom *has* come! Your kingdom *is at hand!* I'm walking in it right *now!* You have already given me the kingdom. Your kingdom is in Me!"

The rhema word that has reawakened, renewed, and rejoiced my soul is this:

*I, as God's child, have the ability to do God's will on earth just as it's already being done in heaven. Jesus' statement, *Thy kingdom come. Thy will be done* isn't a petition. It isn't a request to God. It is a declarative statement of truth, an absolute fact, an authoritative command to the prince of darkness, the father of lies. It is a war cry to the principalities and powers of the air!

*I have the power inside me to subdue the kingdom of darkness on earth.

*I have the mighty authority of God in me to loose, *on this day*, on this earth, what has already been loosed in heaven.

*Being kingdom-minded causes heaven and earth to connect!

*The eyes of God's people are being opened in these last days. His children are beginning to understand that they have been living and walking powerless in their Father's kingdom simply because they have been listening to the lies of the enemy.

*God's kingdom isn't coming. *It has come!* His will isn't going to be done. It *is being* done on earth NOW! It *is being* done by God's mighty army of believers whose eyes have been opened and whose ears have heard the battle cry of the Spirit.

So, rise up, people of God! His kingdom *is* come! It is here *now*! We are living and walking in it *today*! His will is being done by GOD HIMSELF who is living in us!

I will never again pray Jesus' words: *Thy kingdom come. Thy will be done* in the same ineffective, unproductive, powerless way as before. As this mighty truth has begun to soak into my soul, I have taken up my armor anew, having been refreshed by the *living* Word. I have joined the mighty, victorious, last-day army of God's mighty warrior-saints who are, *this very day*, walking in His kingdom and doing His will.

Kingdom of darkness, take heed:

Once I was blind, but now I see
The authority of God abiding in me!
His power in me shows His will being done.
Look out, Darkness: God's Kingdom *has come*!
Glory!

Learning to Lean

One morning, while singing myself awake with that beloved old hymn, *Learning to Lean*, I began to think about the words *learn* and *lean*. It took my morning-fogged mind a moment or two to home in on the fact that the only difference in the appearance of these two words was the letter *R*. I am ever endeavoring to learn. (I think this phrase sounds so much better than 'my brain tends to ping' or 'I have the attention span of a gnat'.) Therefore, since I do endeavor to learn, I began to ponder this observation.

After much pondering, I became firmly convinced of the following facts:

*Worry is a sin.
*One of the desires of my heart is to acquire the ability to constantly *lean* upon Jesus, trusting Him in every circumstance and facet of my life.
Worrylessness is a *learned* ability and not one that God instantly dropped into my soul at the time of my salvation, or even later when I received the baptism of the Holy Spirit.

I, therefore, have decided to enroll in God's course: *Learning to Lean 101.*

During my first class I reviewed scriptures pertaining to *learning*:

The Israelites *learned* to fear God.
The Psalmist *learned* God's laws.
Isaiah had the tongue of the *learned*.
Paul *learned* contentment.
Jesus *learned* obedience.
Jesus said, "*Learn of Me.*"

These words of God led to very encouraging thoughts. But I then remembered that the Word also says it is possible to be 'ever *learning*, yet never able to come to the knowledge of the truth.' Gulp!

I knew from experience how easy it is to read and hear the word of God, preach it during a mountain-top experience, and then go on to some other exciting truth, forgetting I need to practice what I have preached until that truth...that teaching...that *learning* has become a very part of my being.

The Lord then drew my attention to the letter *R* and the startling observation that the simple act of removing the *R* from the word *LEARN* would lead me to my goal...*LEAN*.

I found this extremely interesting!

Now if I could just discover what the *R* represented; it might help me in my quest. I won't bore you with the sum of my discoveries, but with help, from my Teacher, Holy Spirit, I came up with a multitude of *R* words.

Here, in a nutshell, is what I found:

*R*emove *R*ebellion
*R*esist *R*eligion
*R*ebuke *R*ejection

Renounce Revenge
Refuse Reviling
Remember Redemption
Return, Repent, and *Revive Righteousness,* and
Rejoice...
because then I am *learning to lean.*

The assignment is crystal clear. I think it's the homework that's going to take me quite a loooong time to complete. So, Holy Spirit, if You don't mind, I believe I'm going to have to be doing a lot of *leaning* on You while I *learn.*

Listen for the Pings in Life...
They are Worth It

Kathy's First Facebook Post: Let the fun begin.

Kathy's Second Facebook Post: The fun is done.

Kim's Facebook Post: My sister grew the beans, picked the beans, washed the beans, snapped the beans, and canned the beans. Now she has 7 beautiful quarts of canned green beans.

I found the beans, picked up the beans, paid for the beans, and brought the beans home. I now have canned green beans. But I have to admit that hers look a lot cooler on the shelf.

Mom's Facebook Post: I used to *can* many years ago, but now, I no longer *can*. Well, it's not that I can't *can*, I can. I simply no longer choose to *can*. I guess you can say I am a *Has-bean*.

As I was laughing over our Facebook postings, a *pondering* popped into my mind. I had been with my daughters the day before as my youngest began the age-old process of preparing the earth's bounty for future sustenance in the dead of winter when gardens are resting and gathering strength for next year's productions. She was going to *can* green beans and tomatoes from her very own garden.

She had laughingly called her sister and me to come over and visit if we were bored. We, looking for any occasion to get together, appeared on her doorstep ready to cheer her on in her domestic doings. We are very good cheerleaders, so she worked and we cheered. Actually, we did a *wee* bit of bean-snapping and tomato cutting-up. (Please notice the emphasis on the word *wee*.)

The fact that she only had half a bucket of beans and a few tomatoes didn't daunt my fearless, little 'Susie-Homemaker.' She was focused. She was going to can! And we were going to stand by her side and encourage her even though, in our estimation, it seemed like a lot of work for so little gain. Nevertheless, she persevered and, eventually, with the help of her pressure cooker and her sideline superintendents, she became the proud producer of seven jars of appetizingly-beautiful green beans and three jars of cheery, bright-red tomato juice.

As I was pondering this momentous occasion, I asked myself if all her effort was really worth the outcome, and the answer that came to me will probably only be understood by those who have ever engaged in this domestic ritual known as *canning* or the *putting up* of the fruits of their labor.

We sat around the table celebrating her accomplishment with cold, frosty glasses of iced tea. I was still wondering if all the digging, planting, bending, weeding, sweating, picking, washing, snapping, cutting, sanitizing, timing, and careful monitoring of the pressure cooker, to say nothing of the time involved…if all the effort that had gone into this project had really been worth it.

And suddenly, I heard it, the final step in this age-old ceremony which signified the success of the venture. The trumpet sound of victory…

The PING of the lid. A jar had sealed!

As the sound of that tiny PING danced into our ears, all three of us, simultaneously, raised our arms in victory and shouted, "YES!"

Looking into my daughter's beaming face, I saw the answer to my question. YES! *Yes, it had all been worth it!* One small *ping* had been worth all the work that had gone into that one moment of joy.

It's hard to explain the feelings I experienced at that moment, but I will never forget the sound of that *ping*, the shouts of excitement, and the happy, satisfied smile on my daughter's face. That small *ping* had birthed a joy moment in all of us.

Six more joy-filled *ping* moments were to follow, and each one received the same *happy dance* as the very first one had. Life was good.

Later Holy Spirit spoke to me and said, "Peggy, there's a lesson in that *ping*. Life is full of little *pings*. They are all around you. I send them to you daily because I love you. My desire is to bring you the joy of *pings*. You simply have to slow down and listen for them."

"But," He continued, "there is a secret that is associated with those *pings*. The secret is that they most often come after hard, work-wearying tasks that make you wonder if all the effort you're putting into accomplishing a result is really worth it.

Don't ever regret the difficulty that goes into bringing even one small *ping* into the life of someone. That one *ping*, that one moment of joy makes every extra mile, every single hard thing you do for others all worthwhile."

I asked my daughter if I could borrow one of her
jars of green beans for a while.
I taped a little sign on it and put it on my kitchen
counter where I can see it every day as a reminder.
The sign reads: **Listen for the PINGS in life…they are worth it!**

Little Things in Life

Written to my sweet friend, Julie

My Dear Forever Friend,

One Sunday morning in church during the Christmas holidays, I was struggling with deep discouragement when you leaned over and whispered in my ear, "Faith is the victory." Your words hammered at my heart and cracked it open. Faith, in huge gulping breaths began to stream in, forcing out the hard-cold fingers of unbelief and suddenly...

What to my wondering mind should appear?
but peace, faith, and comfort from Jesus so near.

(Sorry, I just can't help myself, it is Christmas time you know.)

Seriously though, I wonder why I'm so amazed when I realize the word of God works. Sometimes I feel like a big DUH! God said it would, and He doesn't lie. So why am I surprised? I'm thinking it's because I have traces of unbelief floating around in my gray matter somewhere. But do you know what? I am determined to flush that unbelief out if it takes a lifetime. Wait a minute, it will! (take a lifetime, that is.) Oh well, that's what life is all about, isn't it? Becoming more and more conformed to the image of our Savior.

Thank you, my sweet friend, for sharing Jesus and His word with me. Thank you for blessing my life. I want to bless you back, so I have decided that for one whole week I am going to be pumping like crazy to fill up your 'soul bowl' with prayers for courage, faith, trust, and peace. I am going to be blessing you with daily joy and contentment, decreeing that each day you will find yourself personally touched with the realization that this very day was made especially for you, by God, your Father, to enjoy every little thing in your life.

Little things like: sudsy dish water, frilly curtains, hot baths, crunchy snow under your boots, birds in your backyard, warm blankets to snuggle under while you watch one of your favorite TV shows, a quiet corner in which to read, time to read, and wonderful books to read, hot chai, toothpaste that makes your teeth sparkle and your tongue tingle, and your breath smell good, hot biscuits and gravy, music that makes you dance, fingers that work, Bible verses that fill your heart with joy.

Vacuum cleaners that gobble up the tiniest specks of dirt, hair spray to help you look beautiful, a pastor to feed your hungry soul Sunday after Sunday, dental floss, friends who love deeply, scissors that actually cut, the ability to laugh in the midst of sorrows, fingernail files, love to give to others even when they don't deserve it, silverware (cause it would be really messy to eat without it), windows that shine in the sunlight, kind doctors, toilet tissue (thank You, Lord, for that), computers that are fast, taste buds, scales to track your weight (no, cross that one off the list), medicine to help your body function better, cute earrings, fuzzy socks, telephones, warm homes, and clocks that remind you to take time to 'taste and see that the Lord is good.'

I will be decreeing these blessings of God upon you and singing over you with joy. So, precious friend, keep trusting Jesus, listening to His words, and sharing them with everyone...

especially me.

Loose Your Tied Colts

s Jesus was preparing to enter Jerusalem, He instructed two of His disciples to go into the village, *find a colt tied*, which had never been ridden by anyone, *unfasten it and bring it to Him*. He said that if anyone asked why they were doing this, they were to answer: The Lord needs it, *and He will send it back here presently*. Mark 11:1-4

While pondering these words from my porch swing early one morning, Holy Spirit quietly spoke to my heart: *Let your tied colt go. Give it to the Lord, now and willingly, and He will send it back presently.*

I began to think of all the tied colts we have in our lives...people, possessions, positions, personality traits, attitudes, 'soulish' characteristics. *Colts* that we consider worth holding onto. *Colts* that belong to us. *Colts* that we can't bear to let go.

God is calling us to *loose these colts*; bring them to Him so He can work on them. If we give Him, willingly, a defiant teen-ager, a job we hate, a home or car that is tying us up financially, a proud attitude that is destroying our relationship with a loved one, or whatever it is that we have tied tightly to ourselves, He promises in His word that He will *send it back to us presently*.

He's telling us to loose it so He can work. He needs it in His hands to work on it. Like the child who asks his father to fix his broken toy, but refuses to let go of it, we ask God for help, then hold tightly to people, possessions, attitudes, and habits, trying to do everything we know how to fix, change, or renew them ourselves. We then wonder why they never get fixed. God is telling us to let go, put our *colts* in His hands, under His control, and let Him fix them.

The disciples did as they were told, and the owners *let their colt go.* Mark 11:7 says, *"And they brought the colt to Jesus, and threw their outer garments upon it, and He sat upon it."*

Sometimes when we have *loosed our colt,* perhaps it's a loved one, it looks as if the world has thrown its garments over him because we see no change, no softening, no renewed life. In the natural our *colt* seems steeped in the ways of the world and appears to be growing even farther away from that which we had hoped, planned, and prayed for so fervently.

Ah, Beloved. You are looking through the eyes of flesh and not the eyes of faith. Notice the last part of verse 7: *and He sat upon it.* Your *colt* may look like the world, wearing the garments of the world; but God is sitting on top of it. Trust Him. He is in control. Let Him work on your loved one, your job situation, your pride, your covetousness, your fear. Take your eyes off your *colt* and put them on the Lord.

Verses 8 and 9 of Mark 11 say that *many threw their garments before Him and cried out praises and blessings to the Lord.* Oh beloved, be one of the many. Take your garments which are your faith, your attitudes, your emotions, your thoughts, your mouth speaking forth faith-filled words and spread them before the Lord. Cry out hosannas, blessings, and praises to Him Who sits on every *colt you have loosed* into His hands. Trust Him to do what He has promised.

It may look as if your *colt* is walking all over your garments, trampling your trust, your hope, your faith, your belief, your very heart into the dust. But remember, you did not throw your garments before the *colt*. You threw your garments before the *Lord, the King of Kings!*

Only spiritual eyes can see that *Almighty God Himself* is sitting on your *colt*. Only spiritual ears can hear His promise: *I will send it back presently...tamed*. Don't be afraid. Trust God. *LOOSE YOUR TIED COLT!*

Loss

My daughter, Kim, has a home business making personalized jewelry. After designing a necklace for those who are grieving the loss of a loved one, she posted this writing on her blog. I feel it is a poignant look at the suffering grief brings. And it is written by one who has crawled through this valley on her hands and knees and come out victorious. It touched me deeply when I read it, and I pray it will touch you also.

We all suffer loss in our lives. It is an unavoidable, unexplainable, unfair fact. I am amazed at the strength of the human heart. I remember days, in the fresh agony of loss, when I wondered how my heart was still beating, how my muscles still made my body go through the everyday motions of life. For that matter, how dare the sun shine so brightly and strangers around me act as if the world is still normal. SO many walk among us with broken hearts, tired eyes, and pasted half-smiles, watching the minutes as they tick into hours that tick into days.

We who watch the grieving comment about how 'strong' they are, how 'brave'— while deep down we know that strength and bravery have little to do with days that are survived simply because their bodies continue to breathe in and breathe out. We long to bring some comfort to an impossible situation, to ease their pain, to somehow fill the emptiness in their hearts and arms.

I believe in the power of prayer. PRAY for the people you love who are grieving. Don't give them platitudes. Don't feel you have to say something just to fill the quiet. Actually, please DON'T! Sometimes silence is the best gift we can give. A hug. A listening ear. That and a month's supply of paper goods. (Gotta love my practical friends!!)

As we mourn, I believe that God holds us in His hand, whispers strength, and waits with us. The screaming pain of grief is often so loud that we can't hear that Voice. And for a time, we may not even WANT to hear it. The heart-wrenching intensity of the finality of a loss often makes us unaware of most of what goes on around us. Many months later we wake up and realize that we *might* be ready to take a tiny step forward, and God opens His hand and gingerly sets us on our feet.

In recent months, too many parents around me have suffered the unimaginable loss of a child. Even after I've held my perfectly formed stillborn son in my arms for one brief hello and goodbye, my heart and mind still can't begin to imagine living through the loss of one of my sons. Two days, fourteen years, twenty-five years, thirty-eight years…**no** amount of time is 'enough' to be with our child, our very heart. Unless we have walked those parents' path, we have no idea of the pain.

As a life-long nurturer, I yearn to ease the pain of those suffering loss. At the same time, I realize that designing a necklace for a grieving mom is a paltry attempt at comfort. A Band-Aid to cover the loss of a limb. But I also hope that it might be a small but visible symbol to the world around them that their child is loved, and missed, every single day.

I have to confess that I hate those 'If Tears Could Build a Stairway' memorial stones. You know the ones? After my husband's funeral several of those stones were brought to our house. I am embarrassed to say that, for some strange reason, they just made me crazy. So, one day I had a very cathartic session of breaking them up and putting them in the trash. I didn't want rocks. I wanted my husband back. I wanted my family to be whole and healthy and happy. For some reason I felt better afterward.

(If you are a dear friend who gave us one of these stones, I AM SO SORRY!!! But please know that they helped…in a more 'non-traditional' way.)

Isn't it ironic that the crazy woman who took out her grief on some well-intentioned garden stones now has the nerve to design a necklace to gift to others who grieve? Some days I don't know what to do with that…which is why my heart is full each time I hear that this small token of remembrance brought even a brief smile to a hurting soul.

I pray that the precious moms, wives, and others who grieve might find some small measure of peace in the jewelry I create.

But if someone decides to toss, damage, stomp on or otherwise dismantle it— I have firsthand knowledge of that being a bit healing too.

Kim Baer

Murmurs in the Midnights

D o we murmur in our midnights? Whine in our wildernesses? These questions marched through my mind as I pondered Exodus 15 and 16. God's people have begun their journey from captivity to the promised land, and after witnessing God's awesome deliverance from their enemy, they rejoice with great jubilation in song and dance. *Life is good! Their joy abounds!*

But in days to come they begin to veer from the direction of their promised land, and now find themselves in a wilderness void of water. Listen! What is that noise rising from the campfires and floating upward toward the heavens? Ah, is it not the whispers of whines in the wilderness? Whines being flung from throats parched with thirst? I wonder? Does the parching come from the lack of water or from the murmurs in the midnight? *Life is bad! Their joy is gone.*

God hears their murmurs and provides waters that flow sweet down their dry throats. An oasis of blessing appears (Elim's springs of water) abundant sustenance, and rest. *Life is good.* Wait! What's that sound? I think it's silence. Where is the rejoicing with great jubilation in song and dance for God's abundant provision? *Life is good, but their joy is absent.*

They come, at length, to the Wilderness of Sin which is located between Elim (Provision from God) and Sinai (Promises from God). Finding themselves trudging through this Wilderness, a small familiar song begins to waft on the midnight breezes. Its crescendo grows. Ah, now the words become distinct. They are recognizable. They are murmurs in the midnight. *Life is bad! Their joy is non-existent.*

God continues to hear their murmurings. Again, He provides. Manna! Food from heaven! But once more...the sound of silence. No singing. No dancing. *Life is good,* but still *their joy is missing.*

More provision. More *Life-is-good* moments, but once again the music of murmuring begins. The whispers of wicked ungratefulness make their way toward the throne of Almighty God.

How long, O God? How long will You listen to these murmurings from Your people? How long will Your mercy and grace enfold them in Your heart of Love? How long until they learn to sing songs of gratefulness and joy? Oh, foolish people. Will they never learn?

As I continued pondering the foolishness of the Israelites, I began to realize just how much like them we are. We find ourselves in the wilderness of dryness, the darkness of fear, and our song becomes rift with the lyrics of the *father of lies.* The words begin as soft sighs and hissing whispers, but soon swirl into whirling waves of insinuation, and we begin to entertain the ugly suspicion that our Father's promises, His precious words, are not true, and *our joy is gone.*

We murmur in our midnights, in our travels through lands of dryness. We embrace un-belief in God's ability to keep us, to hold us, to provide for us. All the while He, in His infinite love, holds forth the very word of life that could bring us joy.

Do we recognize this Word of Life, this Bread from heaven, this *joy* from Jesus or do we, like the Israelites, call out when we receive provision from God's Hand: *Manna? (What is it?)*

Do our souls cry out and leap for *joy* at the goodness of our God when we read in His word, that even though our ungrateful murmurings come before the Lord, He in His compassion and mercy still provides us Bread from heaven? Do we really understand what this means?

Do we hear Him when He tells us to *take as much as we need?* Do we really listen? Or are we in too much of a 'snit' about our circumstances to gather what is so freely offered during our *seasons of 'snitfulness'?*

Are we so focused on our fear, so languishing in our perceived lack of provision that we can't see the proverbial forest for the trees, and we miss the veritable feast our Father has laid out before us even in the very presence of the enemy?

Are we so satiated in our seemingly impossible situation that we fail to heed our Father's gentle voice calling us to take up and eat the manna He has provided? To taste and see that He is good?

Oh, Lord, that we would learn to give no credence to the call to disbelieve Your word; that we would learn to not listen to the taunting voice of hell urging us to whine in the hard places; that we would turn from the lure of the enemy's words tempting us to ignore Holy Spirit's voice quietly calling us to turn away from our vain imaginations and our skepticism of Your promises to never leave us or forsake us.

Help us cross over from our wanderings in the land of confusion and doubt. Plant our feet firmly back in Your kingdom of belief and trust.

Open our eyes and cause us to see the Manna, the Bread from heaven, the Word of Life, the Joy You so lovingly hold out to us in our times of trouble.

    Father,

Cause us, in our times of unbelief, to remember Your faithfulness.

Lead us, in our confusion, to never abandon our place of rest in You and Your promises.

Remind us, when our hearts are empty, to dance and declare Your faithfulness.

Teach us, in perilous times, to turn our fears into shouts of praise for Your protection.

Call us, in our discouragement, to cling to memories of Your provision.

Help us, in our hopeless sorrow, to sing songs of gratitude for Your Presence.

Encourage us, Lord, to not murmur in our midnights.

My Christmas Moment

*E*very year I look for a sign that Christmas has arrived. I call it *My Christmas Moment*

One year it happened as my daughter and I were presenting the song PERFECT LOVE (Mary's Song) in sign language to the ladies at our annual Christmas Gathering at church.

Dressed as angels, we stood beside Hope, our pastor's young preteen daughter who was portraying Mary. She was seated in a rocking chair gazing tenderly at a small, sheet-wrapped doll held gently in her arms. Her baby...Jesus.

Glancing down, I caught a glimpse of little bare toes sticking out from under Mary's robe. They were painted bright orange, and on one big toe was a tiny decorated pumpkin emblem that was beginning to chip around the edges.

As I looked at that little painted toe, suddenly the Christmas story became Alive. Real. Earthy. Poignant.

I was overwhelmed with emotion. I saw, not the glamorized version of sweet-smelling hay and heavenly background music accompanied by the soft lowing of cattle, I saw the actual youthfulness and tender innocence of Mary who had been chosen to be the mother of Jesus… God Himself, in flesh.

A child birthing a Child.

My spirit leapt in awe at the wonder of it. Joy flooded my heart, and suddenly I knew.

A young girl, named Hope, wearing orange nail polish with a chipped outline of a pumpkin on her toe had birthed *My Christmas Moment.*

My Friend Joanie

*L*ately I've been thinking about my friend, Joanie. Missing her. Remembering her. Loving her.

I don't think Joanie set out to list as one of her life's goals being able to make a 'love memory' so deep in the hearts of others that when she moved on from this earth, we would feel as if she left us with a gaping, empty hole of sorrow in our hearts...but she did.

I could list her endearing qualities, but those of us who love her already know them. Those attributes *were* Joanie. They weren't simply wonderful character traits she was trying to emulate. They *were* Joanie. Her love, her personality, her very being was like a 'quiet angel who lifts us to our feet when we have trouble remembering how to fly.' To know Joanie meant to know you were loved.

When our loved ones leave this earth, we hear people say, "No one else can take his or her place." I believe this is true. There will never be another Joanie.

The other day, while reading Psalm 103:15,16: *Our days are like grass, as a flower of the field we flourish. The wind passes over it and it is gone, and its place shall know it no more*, I felt as if God was saying to me, "That's Joanie. I made a special place in My universe just for her. That place is 'Joanie-shaped.' No one else is shaped exactly like her, inside and out. No one will be able to fill that special place ever. I created it once and only for Joanie. And even though she has come

Home, that place will never be filled by another. So, when you hear someone say, 'No one can ever take her place,' they are right. She was special. She was fiercely loved by Me!"

So, My child, take another look at that gaping, so-called empty hole of sorrow you are carrying around inside your heart. It's really not empty you know. It's Joanie-shaped, and she and I have filled it with joy-filled love-memories of her. It's a gift from us to you. We chose each memory especially for you. She and I knew exactly which ones each one of you, her loved ones, would cherish.

I could almost hear Joanie laughingly saying to me, "What are you waiting for? Go ahead, open it. My Father and I know you will love our gift!"

Joy-tears flowed as I bowed my head in prayer: Thank you for these precious memories you've given us to share. I love you, Joanie.

No One Can Take Your Place

My days are as grass, as a flower of the field I flourish. The wind passes over it and it is gone, and the place thereof shall know it no more. Psalm 103:15,16.

As I was reading this Psalm, the word *place* seemed to draw my attention. I closed my eyes and let my thoughts settle in on it. I call it *selah-ing.*

Suddenly I sensed a God lesson building up in my spirit. I stilled my heart, and God began to form His thoughts in my mind.

"Are you hearing the word *place* in your heart?" He asked softly. "Is it standing out to you in your mind?"

"Yes, Lord," I answered.

"Well," He continued, "That is because the word describes you."

"Me?" I whispered.

"Yes, I made a special *place* in My universe just for you. That *place* is Peggy-shaped."

"No one else can fill it. No one else is *shaped* exactly like you...inside and out. No one will ever be able to fill that special place. I created it only once and only for you. Even when I call you *Home*, that place will never be filled by another. So, when people say, *No one else can take your place*, they are right."

I sit in indescribable awe. I am undone.

Oh, how God loves me!

I am special!

I am spatial!* (Tee hee)

*Spatial-occupying; having the character of space

 No Shining Splendor in Your Heart?

Who is among you who reverently fears the Lord,
who obeys the voice of His Servant,
yet who walks in darkness and deep trouble
and has no shining splendor in her heart?

Let her rely on, trust in and be confident in the NAME of the Lord,
and let her lean upon and be supported by her God.

Isaiah 50:10

discovered this scripture when I was going through an extremely difficult time in my life. As I read the first part, I realized it described exactly how I felt. I knew that I loved the Lord with all my heart and tried, to the best of my ability, to listen to His voice and 'walk His talk'.

And yet, I was void of feelings, stumbling through a deep, dark valley, hanging on by a thread, and finding no joy in my heart at all. What was the answer to my sorrow, fear, apathy, self-pity, loneliness, and exhaustion? I felt helpless.

As I continued reading these words of Isaiah, I experienced a tiny spark of hope beginning to flicker in my heart. I felt God personally begin to give me the answer to my struggles as I heard these words,

"Trust Me. You can rely on Me. You can be confident in Me...and in My NAME." He paused, and then whispered ever so softly, "By the way, do you know My NAME?"

"I-I-I'm not sure," I stammered, "I thought I did."

"Well, let Me introduce Myself to you," He gently whispered.

"I AM Jehovah-tsidkenu - The Lord Your Righteousness.
I AM Jehovah-m'kaddesh - The Lord Who Sanctifies You.
I AM Jehovah-shalom - The Lord Who Gives You Peace.
I AM Jehovah-shammah - The Lord Who is Always
Present with You.
I AM Jehovah-rapha - The Lord Who Heals You.
I AM Jehovah-jireh - The Lord Whose Provision Shall Be
Seen by You.
I AM Jehovah-nissi - The Lord Who is Your Banner.
I AM Jehovah-raah - The Lord Who is Your Shepherd.

Whatever you need Me to be, for whatever moment or situation you are in...I AM! You can be confident in My NAME.

Choose the NAME for whatever need you have at the moment and call to Me in faith. I will support you. I will give you strength, courage, faith, peace, joy, and love to overcome, in victory, any enemy who comes to steal, kill, or destroy the *abundant Life* I came to give you. You *can* trust Me. You *can* rely on Me. You *can* have confidence in My NAME.

If you believe Me and do what I am telling you, those who are watching your life will cry out in amazement, 'Behold, who is this coming up out of the wilderness, leaning hard on her Beloved?' It will be YOU, My Child. It will be YOU! Coming up out of your wilderness in victory because you have called on My Name."

Dear Brothers and Sisters in Christ, if this is where you are today, listen to these words of the Lord, your God: call out His NAME in faith, trust in His word, lean hard on Him, and watch what He will do! He will bring you out of the wilderness, and you will once again experience *His shining splendor in your heart.*

NOW Moment Gifts

While talking on the phone with a friend who lives in Florida, I was trying to describe the spell-binding, breath-taking, mind-boggling, speech-stopping beauty of our Indiana first of the year, eight-inch snowfall. Suddenly he interrupted with these words, "Yes, but wait until it starts to melt and gets all muddy and dirty-looking, and those big chunks of gray ice get stuck to the bottom of your car."

"Oh," I laughed, "I know that's coming because I've experienced it before. But right now, I'm basking in the joy of this moment, in the *eyes-can't-get-enough* and *memory-can't-store-the-outrageous-beauty-and-wonder-of-it* moment. I'm living in the *NOW* of it."

After ending the call, I felt the Holy Spirit whisper, "Why don't you do this *basking in the moment* more often in your everyday life?"

"Aha," I thought, "a point to ponder." Why don't I *bask* in the beauty of the *NOWS* in my everyday life? How often do I spoil those *NOWS* by seeing the ugly dirt-covered chunks of ice stuck to the bottom of my future? Why do I so often ruin those God-given, perfect *NOW* moments with negative thoughts?

It's 9 below with a wind-chill of minus 33 degrees. Giant tree limbs are laying in the yard, felled by high winds and the weight of too much snow piled onto their fragile branches. At some point in the future, they will have to be cut up and hauled away. The snow-piled walks will have to be shoveled and the cars dug out. But *NOW* in this very space of time, given to me by God, I am sitting by my fireplace sipping a hot cup of chai and feasting on a snowfall scene so beautiful that words escape me as I try to paint the wonder of it on the canvas of my mind.

I am well aware of what the future fallout from this awesome art-work of the Creator will be, but *NOW* is where I am. *NOW* is where I am living. *NOW* is where my breath is. *NOW* is my gift from God. How do I: Capture it *NOW?* Hold it *NOW?* Live it *NOW?* Bask in it *NOW?*

My pen slowly begins to form the letters *N O W* on my Journal page. Suddenly, in the very center of the *O*, I see, in my mind's eye, a small circle-shaped head portraying a huge, joy-filled smile. As I study it, I realize it is me, and that God is answering my "*How Now?*" question in His very wise, very unique way. He is doing it with an art lesson.

"My child," He said, "you need to practice opening the eyes of your soul to the everyday *NOW Moments* I have given you. When you sense you may be in the presence of one, simply close your carnal eyes, pick up My spiritual paintbrush, and with My hand guiding yours, paint yourself into the very center of that *NOW Moment*. The most important focus of your painting should be the joy-filled smile on your face reflecting the joy of the experience of that moment. The wonderful thing about your work of art will be the fact that you have allowed Me to gently guide your hand as you and I, together, paint your *NOW Moment* from My heavenly perspective."

I then pictured the Lord placing our finished canvas in His holy art collection for His viewing pleasure, sort of like His Book of Remembrance spoken of by Malachi. I saw my painting bringing Him great joy as He sees me capturing His *NOW Moment* gift to me by placing myself right in the middle of it-breathing, tasting, savoring, embracing, experiencing, and praising Him with all that is within me for allowing me to experience, from His perspective, that amazing, incomparable, life-enhancing *NOW Moment*.

Lord, help me capture every *NOW Moment Gift* from You by slowing down, opening my spiritual eyes, and painting myself with a joy-filled smile right in the center of that *NOW Moment*. Teach me to hold it close to my heart.

Ode to a Shopping Cart

A phenomenon especially close to my heart
Is the unfathomable, mystical shopping cart.
Its gleaming body of shining chrome
Is the preponderant subject of this poem.

Each Thursday morning on my shopping day,
I find the carts posed in the same pompous way;
Lined up so stately with all of their friends,
The ones stuck together shrewdly placed at the ends.

Clutching my grocery list, purse, and three kids,
My choice, as usual, has a front wheel that skids.
Out of two hundred carts and eight hundred wheels,
Why do I incessantly choose one that squeals?

I try to act cool as I squeak down the aisles
Ignoring other shoppers' smug, half-hidden smiles.
I know they're rejoicing, so glad that they
Don't have a cart wheel that just turns one way.

When piled high with groceries, it refuses to roll.
No amount of maneuvering, neither push nor pull
Easily moves that cart until it sees my trunk,
Then it quickly glides into my car with a clunk!

I confess to you now, without pride or shame,
My goal in life is neither wealth nor fame.
The inexplicable, secret desire of my heart
Is to someday select...the perfect shopping cart.

Only A Son

Only a mother can know the pain
That a wayward son can give
When he isn't walking in the way
That he was taught to live.

Only the Father can count the tears
That her sorrow-filled heart has shed
In the dark of night when she's all alone
Down on her knees by her bed.

Only a son can stop the deep hurt
And fill her heart with a song
When he says, *I'm coming back home, Mom,
To God...where I belong.*

Our God is an Awesome God!

Every December I begin asking the Lord to lead me to a word for the upcoming year. I began this practice in 2001, and each year He has faithfully brought to my attention a specific scripture to ponder throughout the year.

There was only one year that I couldn't seem to hear Him. The previous year He had given me Psalm 46:10: *Be still and know that I am God.* After much searching, praying, and finally listening, I heard Him say: "My child, you haven't heard My word for the new year because you need to spend more time on last year's word."

Oh! Suddenly, my 'lightning-fast' mind got it. I apparently hadn't learned to *Be still and know* over the last year, so my word for the new one would be Psalm 46:10...*again!*

OUR GOD IS AN AWESOME GOD WHO GIVES US SECOND CHANCES!

In December of 2007, I was led to John 10:10. I remember thinking it was so familiar and hadn't really given my spirit a 'holy jolt' as words in years past had, but I kept bumping into it everywhere I turned. So, on January 1, 2008, I said, "OK., God, I hear You. I don't understand You, but Your ways aren't mine, so I'll make John 10:10 my verse for the year."

Little did I know that just nine days later, those words would become a lifeline for my faith when my dear husband had a heart attack that nearly took his life. During the next two months, as he lay in hospitals, that scripture was my war cry as I stood in the battle for his life: *The thief comes to steal, kill, and destroy; I am come that you might have life, and have it more abundantly!*

OUR GOD IS AN AWESOME GOD WHO KNOWS EXACTLY WHAT WE NEED AND WHEN WE NEED IT!

As I was seeking this year's word, I was drawn to Psalm 26:1 in the Amplified Bible. *Vindicate me, O Lord, for I have walked in my integrity: I have **expectantly trusted** in, leaned on, and relied on the Lord without wavering and I shall not slide.*

Two words caught my attention, and I couldn't get them out of my head: EXPECTANTLY TRUSTED.

I believe this year that God wants me to practice EXPECTANTLY TRUSTING Him. He is calling me to…get in His word, thoroughly believe that He means what He says, and then EXPECTANTLY TRUST that He is going to do what He has said He is going to do.

I am to EXPECTANTLY TRUST Him to show up when I pray!

As I was pondering these thoughts, the Holy Spirit asked me this question, "Have you ever seen a child turn the handle of a *Jack-in-the-Box* and watched the EXPECTANCY on his face as he waited in anticipation for *Jack* to 'pop up'?"

"Yes, I have," I answered.

"Well, I want you to be like that child. I want you to EXPECT Me to 'pop up', to show up in your life every day, everywhere you turn. I have told you in My word that when you seek Me, you will find Me. I have promised I would show up, and I will. I have shown up in the past. I will show up in the present, and I shall show up in the future. All you have to do is keep cranking and EXPECTANTLY TRUST Me to 'pop up' anywhere at any time."

"Learn the song that I am singing, and you will become more skilled in knowing when to expect Me. The slower you turn the crank on the box, the longer it will take for Me to 'pop up.' So, keep cranking and 'crank fast.' The faster you crank, the quicker and more often I will 'pop up'!"

OUR GOD IS AN AWESOME GOD WHO ALWAYS SHOWS UP!

So, I would encourage you, dear ones, to ask God for a word for this coming year, and when He leads you to it, grab hold of it with all of your might. Think on it, ponder it, consider it, sing it, talk it, discuss it, pray it, and meditate on it. If you do this, I promise you will find that...

OUR GOD IS AN AWESOME GOD!

Perfect Love Casts Out All Fear and Worry

I awoke one Saturday at 5:00 a.m. with these words in my mind: *Perfect love casts out all fear*, and within a matter of seconds this scripture became life to me. Without going into great detail, which I am not sure I could do even if I wanted to because it was such an emotional experience for me, I want to try to share with you what the Lord showed me.

I knew this scripture. I had read it, heard it, quoted it, and understood it (or so I thought) for over forty years. But God showed me, in one instant of time, that I had it all wrong. Once again, I, mighty woman of faith, (said with tongue in cheek) had managed to turn one of Father's promises into another 'work.'

"How did you do that?" you ask. "I don't know," I answer, "but I seem to be able to do it quite easily and often."

My interpretation of this scripture has always been this: If I could get my *self* into the right spiritual place where I would be full of perfect love, then I could command all fear and worry in my life to go. I just had to work harder so that *my* love would be perfect.

In one twinkle of an eye, God took the two words *perfect love* (an adjective and a noun), capitalized them, and changed them into a proper noun. (perfect love became ***Perfect Love**...a Person!*)

Perfect Love is just another name for God!

I suddenly saw that it is *not* me doing all I can to try to get my *self* full of God's *perfect love* so that I can then have the power and authority to face the fear and worry and cast it out of my mind. In that split second, I saw that when I am faced with fear and worry, I need to turn to ***Perfect Love*** so that He can cast the fear and worry out of my mind.

Wow! At that moment such a peace came into my heart, and I realized in a much deeper way than I ever had before what it felt like to be loved with *perfect love* by *Perfect Love*! These are the thoughts that were running through my whole being:

Oh, ***Perfect Love***, My Father, My God!
How much you love me!
How much you bless me!
Oh, what You gave up for me! Your own precious Son!
I can never do anything to make you *not* love me! Even if I chose my way into an eternity without You, Your love for me wouldn't change! Your heart would be breaking as You watched me make my final choice to leave You!
Oh, God! Such *perfect love*! I don't deserve it. I don't understand it. But it is mine!

Thank You, ***Perfect Love***, for showing me You are the ***Perfect Love*** that casts out all my fear and worry.

Pick Up Your Stick

few Sundays ago, our pastor's message really spoke to me. It was entitled *What's in Your Hand?* He was describing the interaction between God and Moses in Exodus 4. It went something like this:

"What is that in your hand?" God asked Moses.

"A *stick*," Moses replied. (Well, he actually said a rod, but stick sounded better in the telling of the story.)

After 80 years of living, all Moses had to show for his life was a *stick*!

"Cast it on the ground!" God commanded. He did, and it turned into a *serpent*. Moses ran. (Who wouldn't have?)

"Pick it up," God said. Moses did, and it became a *stick* again. But this time, it wasn't just an ordinary *stick*. It was God's *Stick*. It was holy, and God was going to use it to perform miraculous wonders.

As I was pondering this, I suddenly had a revelation from Holy Spirit: *Just before Jesus ascended to heaven, He said that signs would follow those who believed, and, in His name, they would pick up serpents.* I felt a 'Jesus jolt' in my spirit.

We believers, like Moses, sometimes view ourselves just as he did. All we see are *sticks* in our hands. How many of us look at our lives and think: Is this all I have to show for my life? God, I have nothing of worth to present to You. I have lived all these years and have accomplished nothing, at least nothing big. I had such high hopes, such big dreams, and now…nothing. All I have to show for my life is this *stick*.

How many of us hold *sticks* of: failed marriages, wayward children, dead-end jobs, messed up relationships, financial problems, health issues, missed opportunities, emotional baggage, disappointments, loneliness, hopelessness, and the list goes on. Satan has convinced us that our sticks are worthless. They have no value whatsoever. They are evidences of our failures, our worthlessness, our wasted lives. They are *serpents*.

Children of God, we have bought a lie!

What *stick* do you have in your hand? Your *stick* may look like a worthless mess as you see your broken dreams lying at your feet. All of your hopes have become a *serpent* writhing in the dust, and all you want to do is run away from it all. You see yourself destroyed by the enemy. You see yourself as a washout, a loser, a failure.

But Jesus says, "Believer, cast that *stick* down, give it to Me, and lay it on My altar. Don't run away. Don't be afraid. I will take what you see as your *serpent*, your seemingly failure in life, and I will make it holy. I will give it back to you, but it will no longer be your *stick*; it will be the *Rod of God*!

As Aaron held up the bronze *serpent* in the midst of the Israelites so that all who looked upon it were made whole, you will lift up what *had been your stick* of disappointment: failed marriage, prodigal child, financial disaster, dysfunctional family, health battles, broken dreams, etc. And all the wounded, broken-hearted, weary, discouraged, and hopeless who see it will remember what that *Rod* used to look like, and they will marvel at the miracle God has performed in your life. They will be made whole because of Me and My power.

So, beloved, in My Name, pick up your *stick* (it will not harm you), go out into your world sharing and showing the good news of what I have done for you and your *stick*… remembering My words: *And I, if I be lifted up from the earth, will draw all men to Me." (John 12:32)*

Oh, Holy Spirit, help me pick up my *stick* and watch God change it into *His Rod* and work miraculous wonders in the lives of those who see my Jesus.

Press Through the Crowd

was beginning to feel weary in prayer for my unsaved loved ones when Jesus spoke these words to me.

"My child, do you remember how the woman with the issue of blood told herself that if she could just touch the hem of My garment, she would be whole?"

"Yes, I remember," I answered.

"Do you know what she had to do to get to Me so she could see her prayer fulfilled?"

"Uh, well, uh…," I stammered.

"She had to press through the crowd," He said.

Then the Lord was silent. That's all He said: *She had to press through the crowd.*

His words tumbled through my mind and sank slowly into my heart.

What crowds do I have to press through and shove aside to touch Jesus, so I can see my prayers for my loved ones fulfilled?

As I pondered this spirit and soul splitting question, a list of my own personal crowds began to clearly come into view...

*Unbelief (my own and that of others)

*Apathy (laziness)

*Cynicism (even anger)

*Discouragement (hopelessness)

*Weariness (spiritual and physical)

*False teachings (collected from many sources)

*Ignorance (sometimes caused by my pride)

*Lies of the enemy (sometimes from loved ones)

...I stopped before the crowd grew larger.

"Oh, Lord," I sighed. "That's a very big crowd. Do You have any tips on crowd-control?"

"Yes," He answered. "Do what she did:

*Keep your eyes on the goal which is the hem of My garment. (To do that you must stay low; humble yourself.)

*Press on in faith. (Keep your ears open, always listening to My words because that is how faith comes.)

*Shove aside, with determination, whoever or whatever gets in your way. (Be not afraid of their faces.)

*Don't let the size of the crowd frighten you. (Remember Gideon and his three hundred men.)

*Wait with hope and expectation. (Because I do keep My promises.)

*Press through the crowd. (Keep on keeping on.)

Then you will touch the hem of My garment and see your prayers fulfilled."

My weariness vanished.

Pssst! Have You Heard the News? Mary is Pregnant!

Pssst! Have you heard the news? Mary is pregnant! So went the gossip among the town wags at the well some two thousand years ago, and it all began when these words were whispered by a young girl named Mary:

Lord, let it be unto me according to Your word.

These well-known words from Luke 1:38 struck a chord in my heart as I was reading Mary's response to the angel's message from God. Questions began to tumble into my imagination.

What if, when encountering my present personal circumstances, instead of listening to others tell of the impending pitfalls, failures, and disasters suffered by them in the same situations, I listened to the voice of the Holy Spirit breathing the promises of God's word into my heart and then proclaimed faith-filled words like Mary?

Lord, let it be unto me according to Your word.

What if my responses to terrorist news broadcasts, negative doctors' reports, disasters, joblessness, etc. were governed, not by the natural knee-jerk emotions of my soul and flesh, but by the super-natural power of Holy Spirit-filled words spoken by Mary?

Lord, let it be unto me according to Your word.

What if I allowed God's presence to overshadow me so completely that my trust in Him would fill me to overflowing with expectation in the faithfulness of His promises, and my first response to any difficult situation in my life would echo the words of Mary?

Lord, let it be unto me according to Your word.

What if, during this holy season of Christmas, I, like Mary, could walk *pregnant* with the expectation of God's word being manifested in my life daily? What if, at every turn, I trusted His love for me enough to breathe the words spoken so long ago by Mary?

Lord, let it be unto me according to Your word.

Hope began to rise in my heart. I bowed my head and prayed, "Oh Father, I want to be *pregnant* this holy season.

Lord, let it be unto me according to Your word.

Suddenly, I heard whispering in heaven, "Pssst! Have you heard the news? Peggy is *pregnant!*"

May this blessed Christmas season find us all...pregnant!

Put on Jesus

Have you ever had one of these thoughts cross your mind?

Eat those cookies...you can diet tomorrow.
Pass on that gossip (oops, I mean information) about someone...it's too good to keep to yourself.
Skip your exercise for today...you're too tired.
Don't volunteer to do that...it will take too much time and effort.
Put that phone call or hospital visit off...you can do it tomorrow.
Buy that expensive outfit...you are worth it.
Take that nap...you can finish this job another time.
Watch that TV program...you can read your Bible later.
Go to that R-rated movie...it only has a couple of sex scenes and a few bad words in it.
Sleep in...you can miss church today because it's really cold, and you need to watch your health.
ad infinitum...

Clothe yourself with the Lord Jesus Christ and make no provision for indulging the flesh.
Romans 13:14

As I was reading the above scripture, I heard myself asking my Self this question: Self, how do I go about, practically, making no provision for indulging my flesh?

I know what the words *provision* and *indulging* mean, but when I am pondering a scripture, I like to look up definitions and synonyms for familiar words. So, I called on my iPhone friend, Siri.

Provision means arrangement or plan.

Indulging means to cater to, coddle, pamper, gratify, nourish, give in to, or please.

So now I rephrase the question to my Self: Self, how do I, practically, put a stop to *giving in to* and *nourishing* the ungodly *plans* that my physical nature wants me to engage in?

I find it encouraging that God doesn't tell me to stop thinking about those evil desires (ungodly plans) *before* He gives me instruction on how to stop. He says I am to clothe myself with the Lord Jesus Christ *first*, and *then* stop thinking about the evil cravings my physical nature or flesh desires.

This brings up a new question for Self: Just how do I go about actually doing this *putting on of Jesus?*

Back to my friend, Siri. I find two definitions of *putting* :

#1. assigning a value to.

#2. moving to or placing in a particular position.

I know this may seem strange, but suddenly those two definitions answered my question.

Definition #1 *Assign a value to.* When tempted to indulge my flesh, I need to remember, think about, and focus my mind on the *value* of my Lord Jesus Christ. He is my Savior, my Master, and my inti-mate Friend. I need to consider Who He is, what He has done for me, and my constant need for Him. I must ponder His passionate love for me, His goodness, His mercy, and His undeserved grace. I must answer this question:

What is Jesus' *value* to me?

Definition #2 *Moving to or placing in a particular position.* As I attempt to make everything all about me and my wants, I must place Jesus, the Lord of Lords and the King of Kings in the *position* He belongs; high and lifted up, exalted above everything in heaven and on earth and under the earth. I must ask myself this question:

Where have I *positioned* Jesus in my life?

Words of an old familiar song began flowing through my mind. Only this time the words became extremely poignant and personal.

If I first turn my eyes upon Jesus and look fully at His face only, then the things of this world (my fleshly desires) will become dim as I walk and live in the light of His glorious grace.

I must *fix my gaze on Christ and only glance at my fleshly cravings.* (Colossians 3:2)

This, to me, is God's *provision* of a practical way I can *put on Jesus.*

If I *first* walk after the leading of the Spirit, I will not indulge the desires of my flesh

Red Light, Green Light

While driving to school one morning, I pulled up to a stoplight and stopped. As I looked over at the car beside me, I noticed it slowly inching its way into the intersection. I realized the driver was expecting the light to change to green at any minute, but his anticipation was a bit premature. The light remained red, yet he continued to slowly roll forward.

I was wondering if he was going to continue forward or stop and wait until the light actually turned green. He finally decided to brake, and just as he came to a complete standstill, the light changed. The traffic around him surged forward, but he didn't move. I wondered if his reflexes were slow or if his engine had died. I gave a little chuckle to myself thinking he was probably not a very 'happy camper' at this moment.

As I proceeded on my merry way, I noticed in my rearview mirror that he had finally started moving forward. Meanwhile, the cars that had been beside him, and even some that had been behind him, were now quite far ahead, including *yours truly*.

Suddenly, the Lord brought this thought to my mind: That car is like a lot of Christians, myself included. We have a goal in sight, and we are on a roll for the Lord. We want to do big things for Him, and we're pretty sure we know exactly what He wants us to do, how He wants us to do it, and when we are to do it. We keep saying, "Lord, I'm ready. Let's go. Come on. Change that red light to green. It's time. Give me the 'Go' signal. And we start to inch forward on our own. Though God hasn't given us the green light yet, we continue to slowly roll forward knowing that He is, at any second, going to give us the 'Go' signal.

I've been that car. Have you? There have been times I believe I have heard so clearly what God wants me to do, and I'm willing and ready to do it. The only problem is He hasn't given me the green light. But I don't want anyone else to get ahead of me because, after all, I am VERY spiritual, and how would it look if others got to the place I'm intending to go before I get there? (Pride goes before a 'stall'.) Therefore, I roll forward and begin my one-woman-soft-shoe tap dance on and off the brake as I cast anxious glances toward the light. The loud blast of a horn sends a message to my brain: GO! A still, small voice whispers: Wait on the light.

OK, Lord. I get the message. I need to wait until You give me the green light. Help me, Father! I don't want to be so focused on my own time schedule concerning Your work that when You actually give me the 'go-ahead' signal, I'm so unaccustomed to Your timing that I'm not prepared. This can leave me in a difficult situation, stranded in a perilous intersection with a vision that has died and with reflexes that aren't quick enough to rescue me from danger.

My engine (my energy and enthusiasm) may stall, taking me longer to move forward when You, in Your sovereign timing, turn the light green. My reflexes and my ability to make wise judgments may be so confused from my erratic 'to stop or not to stop' decisions that I come to a complete standstill making me a perfect target for a collision with some other *I-am-running-for-the-Lord-on-my-own-time-schedule Christian*, putting both of us out of commission and out of the race.

Oh, Lord, I wonder how long it will take me to learn to obey Your traffic signals?

Renewing My Mind

I once read that the obedient always obey God when He *first* speaks, and it is those people He will use to make the world know that there is a God. I would love to be one of 'those people', a woman of God who always obeys Him when He *first* speaks.

I know the Lord says His sheep hear His voice. I know I am one of His sheep. I know He would not have said I could hear His voice if He knew it would be impossible for me to do so. I also know one must *first* be quiet enough to hear Him speak. (Do you know how difficult that is for me?)

One of the hardest things for me to do is to still my body, let alone my mind. It seems I am so often fidgeting or moving some body part, swinging a leg, or scratching some un-seeable, unreachable itch. If I do manage to bring all outward body parts under control, there's always the biggest culprit of all - my mind. It's so busy *pinging* here and there and everywhere that sometimes it's gone completely, and I haven't even missed it. I'm sure you've heard the saying about someone or something having a *mind of his/its own*. Well, I often think my *mind* has a *mind of its own*. I have asked the Lord these two questions many times over the last 50 years: How can I change? How can I learn to stop *pinging*, slow down, be still, and hear You better? I would like to share with you some of my ponderings and perceptions I've gathered from God about this *renewing of the mind* business.

I believe that at my creation, my mind was new, fresh, uncontaminated, unspoiled, and probably a state-of-the-art marvel, but unfortunately all that changed. Actually, it didn't take long for the degeneration to begin. Before I could even form the words to express what was going on in that little mass of gray matter in my cute little baby head (at least my mother thought it was cute), I was caught up in the world of *self* and what seemed to be best for my own *self*'s interest. Thus, the newness and freshness of my mind began its erosion.

It continued until that day in 1967, when I heard the words of God telling my heart that if I didn't want to be the way I was, and do the things I was doing, He could help me. If I wanted to stop being superficial and following the ways of the world, I could be changed (transformed) by re-newing my mind. (Romans 12:2) What a revelation! An awesome wonder! Amazing joy began to fill my heart! I felt overwhelmed by that promise, but was so ready to begin the journey of renewal... and what a journey it has been.

Holy Spirit and I have been working diligently to accomplish this transformation for 50+ years. Even though God has given me my own special tutor (His Holy Spirit, without whom I could not spiritually understand any of His words or achieve this goal) this has been no *cake walk*. I have had to discipline my *Self* to slow down, sit down, still my *ADD* body, and quiet my *OCD* mind. (The *OCD* mind thinks everything must be in place, conditions must be perfect, all work done, etc. before I begin this renewing of the mind task, and the *ADD* body parts are on constant alert to spring into action whenever *OCD* mind says: *Let's Move!*)

Discipline means to train oneself to do something in a controlled and habitual way. Some definitions add the words: using punishment to correct disobedience. I don't believe God uses punishment to make me renew my mind because punishment doesn't make me want to slow down, be still, and get into God's word for the right reason. I fear punishment, therefore, it might make me slow down, be still, and read God's word; but the reason I would be doing it would be because of fear and not because I want to be reading it.

I have learned that Satan knows once I begin to get into God's word and catch glimpses of the *goodness* that awaits me in the kingdom of God, I will want what I see. I will want to change my thoughts and my ways because what I see in the word about kingdom living will make me want to experience it, taste it, enjoy it. and possess it. The enemy knows I will turn willingly and joyfully to God's word, hungrily feeding on it, and becoming more focused on the goodness of God and less focused on the attractions of the world around me.

So instead of centering in on distractions that pull me away from renewing my mind, I have purposed to fix my attention on the *goodness* of God and the amazing benefits of walking daily in *kingdom thoughts, kingdom gifts,* and *kingdom living.* With every new revelation of the *kingdom of God* that is brought to me by Holy Spirit, I begin making adjustments in my mind so that my thoughts will line up with each new understanding and perception of God's truths. I begin turning away from kingdom-of-darkness thinking and living, and I begin plunging headfirst into the arms of Jesus and His life-breathing words about *kingdom thinking and living.*

I no longer have my eyes, ears, mind, and body parts tuned in to the enemy's spin on what is important. My former ADD mind and OCD body have become filled with longing to be remodeled, revamped, reconstructed, and renewed because I now have my mind turned from the enemy's alluring traps and my eyes fixed on the prize...the *goodness* of God and His *kingdom living!*

So today, the message of the words in the familiar song *Turn Your Eyes Upon Jesus* has taken on new meaning for me. As I have turned my eyes upon Jesus in the Word of God and looked steadfastly into His wonderful face, the distractions of this world have grown strangely dim as He has renewed my mind and revealed to me the *Light of His Glory, His Grace, and His Goodness in His kingdom living.*

Rescue 91:1

*H*ave you ever wondered why the enemy seems so determined to steal your joy? One moment your heart is filled with the oil of gladness; then, without warning, you wake up to discover those bubbles of bliss have seemingly burst, leaving in their wake an empty dullness.

What's happening? What's really going on here? Simply put, the devil has lowered the checkered flag, and his minions are racing to carry out their assignment against you. The first blow in the battle has landed, and the target, it seems, is your joy.

The devil is after your joy, but his real target is your strength. He knows that the joy bubbling forth from your life has its roots buried deep in the soil of God's strength in you. The *Joy* of the *Lord* is your *Strength*. (Nehemiah 8:10)

If he can poison your joy, he can get to the source of his venomous hatred which is God's Strength living and working in you. Satan's plan is to destroy your precious strength, rendering you helpless, hurt, and hopeless; then move in for the kill.

So how can we fight this enemy who wants to steal our joy, quiet our voice, destroy our strength, and make us cower in fear rather than stand and fight? How can we rise up in full battle mode when we feel our joy slowly slipping through our shaky fingers? How do we stand when we know that keeping our joy amidst the storms of life means all-out war every day for the rest of our lives? Just what is the battle plan God has for us?

God's Battle Plan to RESCUE Our Joy

Step #1 Remember our feelings are not God. God is God. Our feelings do not define truth. God's word defines truth.

Step #2 Remember we are not fighting alone. God is with us and has already declared us winners. (Rom. 8:37)

Step #3 Dial 91:1 RESCUE. Listen very carefully to the instructions, follow them, and then wait. Wait expectantly. Expect to see God Himself rise up and RESCUE you.

(Let's listen in to a previously recorded call for help from a joyless saint.)

Holy Spirit: This is 91:1 RESCUE. Holy Spirit speaking. What is your problem?

Caller: I seem to have lost my joy and don't know how to get it back. Please help me!

Holy Spirit: Just keep calm, remain on the line, and follow My instructions. Do you understand?

Caller: Yes. I understand.

Holy Spirit: O.K. Listen up now. Go to the secret place you share with God and stay put. Being there will keep you stable. Your emotions won't control you. You'll be safe under His protection because no enemy of His or yours can withstand His power. (Psalm 91:1)

Now, simply follow this six-step RESCUE plan:

R Rise up. Lift up your eyes. Look up to Jesus. He is sitting at the right hand of your Father waiting to increase your strength and raise your faith so high that you will feel as if you are soaring with wings like an eagle. (Isaiah 40:26, 29-31)

E Extol His Name. Begin thanking Him for all He has done for you and for all He will do for you according to His promises in His word. The more you thank Him, the more praise will rise up within you. The devil hates hearing praises to God because he knows that God Himself inhabits the praises of His people, and he doesn't want an encounter with God. He will flee in terror. (Ps. 22:3)

S Seek His Face. God says: If you seek Me with your whole heart, you will find me, and when you find Me, I will release you from captivity. So, if you are joyless and feel the enemy has imprisoned you, look diligently for the Lord, and when you find Him, He will set you free. (Jer. 29:12-14)

C Call on His Strength. He clearly tells you in His word, *I am your strength. I am the saving strength of My anointed.* (And guess what? You are His anointed.) (Psalm 28:8)

U Unleash His Word. Build up your faith. Lift yourself up by praying in the Holy Spirit. (Pray in tongues) Your faith will become stronger simply by hearing the word of God, so don't keep silent. Speak out. Talk to yourself, even answer yourself if you want. I promise your faith will grow. (Jude 20; Acts 18:9; Rom.10:17)

E Expect Him. Anticipate His RESCUE. Say to your soul: Soul, we are going to wait on God only. My hope and my expectation are from Him and Him alone because He has told me to wait expectantly on Him, and He will save me. I believe He will fulfill with His hand what He promises with His mouth. So, Soul, we are going to wait...expectantly! (Ps. 62:5; Prov.20:22; II Chron. 6:4)

Holy Spirit: Are you still on the line? How are you doing? Do you understand all of the instructions?

Caller: Yes, yes. I'm here. I've been listening carefully, Holy Spirit, and I've followed all your instructions. Thank you so much. Sorry to cut you off so quickly, but I've got to go...I'm expecting God to show up any minute now! Talk to you later.

Holy Spirit: Well, Father...another successful RESCUE!

Rise Up People of God and Rehearse It in Your Ears

A few weeks ago, our pastor spoke about not holding on to the bad things from our past, but remembering all the good things God has done for us. As he spoke, I was reminded of something I had learned from the Lord a few years before about remembering the good things He does in our lives.

Since I so often need to be reminded anew of *Old* God Lessons and am facing some 'Amaleks' (enemies) in my life, I want to share what God had shown me about remembering the good things He has done.

"…rehearse it in the ears of Joshua, that I will utterly blot out the remembrance of Amalek from under heaven." Exodus 17:14

Joshua had just won a mighty battle against the enemy, yet Moses was instructed to *rehearse* the victory in the ears of Joshua.

Rehearse means to say or do something over and over until you remember it by heart.

Joshua may have just experienced a powerful victory over the enemy, but I believe God is saying that unless he hears the words describing that victory repeated over and over in his mind, that victory will not become a remembered TRUTH in his heart.

*A TRUTH that is so deeply embedded that nothing can shake it.
*A TRUTH that tells him God has given him power to overcome the enemy.
*A TRUTH that proclaims he is a victor in all warfare against the enemies that come against God and him.

The Bible tells us that faith comes by hearing the word of God, so if we want to be powerful men and women of faith, we must learn to rehearse in our ears the mighty victories that God has promised us in His word and that He has previously fulfilled in our lives.

God has said: I will utterly blot out, completely remove, the remembrance of your enemies (your Amaleks) from under the heavens. And God does not promise something He will not deliver.

II Chronicles 6:4 says: God will fulfill with His hands what He promises with His mouth, BUT we must believe that what He says is true! It is imperative that we put our faith in His Word… His promises!

How do we do this? We *rehearse in our ears* His powerful words, His mighty deeds, and His faithful promises. We think them, read them, talk them, write them, sing them, pray them, heed them, remember them, ponder them. When we do this…FAITH COMES!

Faith comes because we have made Him and His word our focus. Any memory of the alleged power of the enemy over us is utterly blotted out from under the heavens. It simply disappears from our minds. There is no longer room in us for thoughts of defeat or fears of powerlessness when facing our enemies because the mighty faith of the Lord of Hosts has arisen in our hearts. We, like Joshua, mow down and disable our enemies with the sword...the Word of God! (Ex.17:13)

So, people of God, as fellow *rehearsers* and *rememberers,* let us *rise up and rehearse in our ears* the powerful words of our awesome Lord! Let us become mighty men and women of God!

LET'S RISE UP, REHEARSE, AND REMEMBER!

 Roses in My Storm

alking in deep sorrow is like looking through a rain-pelted window into a flower-laden garden. I know beauty is there. I've seen it. Touched it. Experienced it. But in the storm, I see only the gray outlines of life.

Colors dim. Fragrances wane. The loveliness is gone.

The rain of my tears has locked arms with the tears falling from heaven. My sight fails. My faith falters.

In the dull grayness of my sorrow, my seemingly sightless eyes glimpse a tiny rose standing alone in a small crystal vase on the corner of my desk. One single rose plucked from its outside world to be placed in my life for such a time as this.

As I gaze at the beautiful color of that lone rose, I sense a tiny flutter of hope stirring from somewhere deep within. My fingers caress the velvety petals as I realize this one special rose was chosen just for me by my Father in heaven to help breathe hope into my soul and bring a tiny ray of light into my sorrowing spirit.

A hope that someday this storm that is hurling sheets of blinding pain against the windows of my heart will dissipate, and the cold gray outlines of my life will begin, once again, to bloom with color.

This one small rose whose life has been cut short has fulfilled the calling for which it was created. God knew, from its inception, what its purpose would be—to bring light and hope to me in the midst of my storm.

Thank You, Lord, for the roses in my life.

For now, we see through a glass darkly...but someday we will know... (I Corinthians 13:12)

Written for my dear friend, Donna, in remembrance of her precious daughter, Sandy

Sea Gulls

ne day, while sitting on our patio in Florida, I watched as a flock of seagulls swept gracefully down to the lake and quickly skimmed the surface filling their mouths with fresh water. They then soared off toward the cliffs of white clouds.

Suddenly the Lord broke into my reverie with these words: "Did you know they are called sea gulls because they spend most of their lives in a sea environment?"

"Yep." I answered, then paused. "Sorry, Lord, I didn't mean to sound flippant, but I already knew that."

"Of course, you did," He laughed. "That's because you're so sagacious." I smiled proudly.

"Did you also know that they often leave the roar of the ocean and fly to the calm stillness of a lake to drink of the fresh water before heading back to their daily lives? Lives that are filled with tumultuous winds, pounding ocean waves, and a seemingly never-ending search for food to fill up the emptiness within them?"

I continued to watch as the last gull disappeared in the distance. I pondered. My heart gave a little Holy Spirit happy hop. "Lord, do You want to know something?" I asked.

"Of course, I do. You know I'm always interested in your ponderings."
I could feel Him smiling at me.

"I was thinking that maybe I should be a little more like those
sea gulls."

"Oh, and how's that?" He chuckled.

"Well, perhaps I, like the sea gulls, need to come away from the
hustle and bustle of my life to the stillness of Your living water.
Maybe I, too, should skim, or better still, take great big gulps of
the fresh, life-renewing waters of Your Word. I'm pretty certain
that that *Word-gulping* would give me the much-needed strength
that would enable me to face the winds and waves of my daily life."

I could feel God's pleasure washing over me. He was smiling, and in
my heart, I heard the gentle voice of Jesus whispering: *Come away
to Me, My child. Each day, wind your way to My calmness. Leave the
busyness and noise behind. Swoop into My Presence and drink of My
fullness: My peace, My joy, My love, My strength, My courage, My
faith...whatever you need. Drink from My lake of fresh Living Water,
and you will be filled with all you need to soar upward as you head back
into your sea of life.*

I climbed onto His lap, settled snugly into His love, and reached
for my Bible. I was suddenly very thirsty.

Seal of Approval

While reading James 1:2-4, the Lord spoke these words to me, "When you are going through a trial, you should consider it a joyful thing that your faith is being proved and tested. (Proved and tested means the process used when a new product or piece of steel is tested or proved to show that it is strong and can stand up under severe conditions and function in the purpose for which it was created.) It should be a joyful realization that your faith is working and doing just what I intended it to do as you are going through a trial. How do you feel about this?" He asked.

"Well," I replied, "I believe it is true because You say it, but it's a hard word. I know it's how I should feel, but I don't always. It's hard to put what I know in my head and my heart into practice in my life."

"You must remember that the enemy has called forth the trial, but I will call forth My *Faith* that is in you, and My *Faith* that is in you will call forth three mighty helpers: *Endurance, Steadfastness, and Patience.* They will be assigned to your case, and along with My *Faith* that is in you, they will do a thorough work on the enemy and his pitiful excuse of a trial.

Suddenly I pictured God saying to me, "Come here, My child, climb up on My lap, lean back upon My chest in trust, and feel the beat of My heart pulsating My peace throughout your entire being. Then watch, in complete peace, and see what a thorough job *they*

(My *Faith* that is in you and its helpers: *Endurance, Steadfastness, and Patience)* will do for you and in you during this testing."

"As you see them victorious (enduring steadfastly with patience), the realization that you will emerge from this battle as a conqueror will begin to sink deeply into your soul. You will be a conqueror with no defects, and you will be lacking in nothing because it is My plan and My way of making you perfectly and fully developed. This truth and the power it brings will allow you to march on with confidence through anything the enemy throws at you."

" I allow this testing process of your faith into the trials that the enemy brings upon you to show *you* that your faith (My *Faith* that is in you) can stand the testing and will come out qualified and stamped with My *seal of approval* which reads…"

THIS FAITH HAS BEEN TESTED AND PROVED:

ENDURING, STEADFAST, PATIENT, QUALIFIED TO STAND UP UNDER SEVERE CONDITIONS, ABLE TO FUNCTION IN THE PURPOSE FOR WHICH IT WAS CREATED, AND GUARANTEED TO BE VICTORIOUS IN TRIALS.

APPROVED by GOD

Seeking God's Wisdom

esterday I came upon a list of twelve people in the Bible who were called *wise*. I was particularly drawn to three of them as I read the descriptions of how they practiced wisdom: Joshua, David, and Abigail.

Joshua

Joshua learned by observing Moses. The first thought that comes to mind when I think of Joshua is his bravery, his courage in fighting battles against the enemy. But as I read about how he gained wisdom, I realized that before he ever became a brave and mighty warrior, he became a humble learner. He sat at the feet of Moses.

To *sit at the feet* of someone means we must place ourselves, positionally, lower than they are. It means we must be willing to listen and glean from them the wisdom of God they have acquired through the years. It means we must not only listen, but watch their wisdom in action by observing them as they *walk their talk*.

We must lower our own opinion of ourselves and lift them higher by honoring them. We must learn to listen to God's wisdom pouring from the lives of those who love, obey, and serve God with passion. We must then practice walking and living in the wisdom of God as they do.

Sitting at the feet, spiritually speaking, of those who daily demonstrate the wisdom and power of the Lord can help us become wise like Joshua.

David

David never let his failures keep him from his God who is the Source of Wisdom. In spite of his many failures, God called David *a man after His own heart.* No matter how far David fell, his heart always loved God.

How encouraging this statement is to me. Reading it reminds me that, in spite of my many failures and my daily stumbles and falls, *nothing* can keep me from my God. Our God looks on our hearts. He knows our love and desire for Him. He doesn't weigh our failures; He weighs our hearts.

The hearts of born-again believers are filled with love and adoration for their God. This truth was settled at the cross the day they looked up from their humble state and took God at His word, the day they accepted Jesus' sacrifice for them and their sins.

On that day His love for them was signed, sealed, and delivered straight to their hearts. Now, in spite of their feelings, or lack thereof, they know their God loves them; and because they know He loves them, they love Him. They believe they are seekers 'after God's own heart,' and like David, they endeavor to never let their failures keep them from the Source of Wisdom...God.

Abigail

Abigail managed her household (her life) with godly wisdom in spite of her circumstances. She knew when to act, when to speak, and when to keep quiet. As I read her story in I Samuel 25, the Holy Spirit reminded me that God's wisdom can keep me living in victory no matter what my circumstances might be.

She humbled herself at the feet of David, who was soon to become the king of Israel, and spoke the truth in wisdom. Then, after being shown favor by David, she returned home to her less-than-perfect circumstances assuming nothing would ever change. Life would continue as usual. Little did she know the blessings her godly wisdom would bring her in the very near future.

Father, the desire of our hearts is to seek You and Your wisdom, so help us:

*to humbly sit at the feet of Your saints gathering Your Words of Wisdom,

*to never let our failures keep us from seeking You and Your Wisdom,

*and to use Your Wisdom to walk victoriously in whatever circumstances we find ourselves.

Servanthood 101

For so is the will of God: that with well doing, as a <u>servant</u> of God you may silence the <u>ignorance of the foolish</u>... I Peter 2:15,16 (Paraphrased by me)

Servant: One who serves; one who performs services for a personal employer.

Servant: One whose purpose is to comply with demands and commands in an attempt to satisfy the desires of others.

Servant: One who engages in an action associated with hard work, dirty hands, other people's messes, and, oftentimes, thanklessness on the part of the recipient.

Servant: A word describing a position the world labels as low-class; a "less-than" word; a negative, derogatory, often demeaning title; a 'justa' as in, "Oh, I'm 'justa' servant."

Servant: A *life course*, never to be found listed in the curriculum of any university, and definitely not a career choice that parents encourage their children to pursue.

And yet...**JESUS TOOK UP A TOWEL**

Ah, a new definition emerges:

Servant: **JESUS.**

Oh, Father, forgive me. I am one of the *ignorant foolish*. I am a snob. I don't want to be. I don't intentionally mean to be. Comparing myself to others, I'm probably not the worst snob in the group, but when I run 'smack-dab' into Your word in the early hours of the morning on my porch swing, it doesn't really matter what number I am assigned as I stand in the line edging its way toward the hierarchy of snobbery. I am still one of the *foolish ignorant*. I am still a snob.

I have elevated certain positions in the world over others. I am *ignorant*. I am *foolish*. I am ashamed. I, like Paul, cry out, "O wretched man (woman in my case) that I am! Who shall deliver me from this *snobberyism*? I, also like Paul, know the answer. PRAISE GOD! HE WILL!

You see, God knows that I am a snob in my soul and flesh only. I am not in my spirit because I am a new creation, and my spirit is 100% Jesus, and Jesus is *not* a snob! God knows my heart and the desire of it. I believe He will lead me in the way I should go, and He will teach me to renew my mind so that my soul will line up with my *snob-free* spirit. It will then be two against one (my spirit and soul against my flesh), and my flesh will just have to get on board.

When that happens, I will no longer be conformed to the world's ways and standards in the study and practice of *snobberyism*. Hallelujah! My *foolish ignorance* will be silenced.

So, Father, please sign me up for *Servanthood 101* and...HAND ME A TOWEL!

#

once heard a Christian described as simple, direct, and unso-phisticated. I would so very much love to be described with those words, wouldn't you?

While reading Psalm 34 today, I am stuck on the words in verse one: *His praise shall continually be in my mouth.* (Continually means constantly; not interrupted) I wonder what it is that keeps praise from continually flowing forth from my lips? I find my answer in verse two:

My life makes its boast in the Lord.

Gulp! My life does not make its boast *in the Lord*. It makes its boast *in me*. I am too focused on myself in almost every area of my life. My source of pride is ME: *my* words, *my* accomplishments, *my* cleverness, *my* kindness, *my* thoughtfulness, *my* appearance, *my* thoughts, ad nauseam. My soul almost feels physically sick as I write the preceding list of *mys*. The list could go on and on, but it's too disgusting, too sickening, and too heavy a burden to bear all at once, so I stop.

In Psalm 67 (my personal word for this year) the words *Let the peoples praise You (turn away from their idols)* appear twice. During my first several readings of these words, I had glossed over the parenthetical phrase containing the word idols. I remember thinking that *someday* I would delve more into the study of idols, figuring I might have a few of them hanging around the fringes of my life.

But God. (This is a phrase that shows up more and more the longer I walk with Him.) *But God* seemed to want that *someday* I had been thinking about to appear sooner than I had planned, and He wanted it to be taken more seriously than I had previously intended.

Lord, I believe, in Your wisdom and love, that You wanted me to focus *first* on verse one in Psalm 67 so I would come to know, without a doubt, that You love me deeply, passionately, and fiercely, and that You delight in me. You wanted me to realize Your face shines on me, and I make You smile. I believe You wanted me to really grasp these truths *because* this year is going to be one of *going deeper in You.*

To *go deeper in You* means I am going to have to get rid of more of *me* so that I can discover more of *You.* To rid myself of more of *me,* I am going to have to recognize and face, head on, the *me* parts that must go, so that the *You* parts can shine forth.

But, Oh Lord, I have known, nourished, and loved these *me* parts for so many years. It is going to be overwhelmingly difficult to say good-bye. It's going to be very painful, in fact. But God, I do want my life to *make its boast in You.* So, where do I begin?

This is what I heard the Spirit of God speak to my heart:

My child, you have been walking around trying to be a gold-plated piece of silver.
(Silver signifies redemption)

Huh? What do You mean, Lord?

Don't you know that I have redeemed you? That I, your God, am living in you, and I am 100% Pure Gold?

Yes, Lord, I-I-I think I know that!

Then why are you working so diligently trying to cover your silver (your redeemed soul) with a thin layer of gold? Why are you trying so hard to appear perfect? Why don't you just be simple, direct, and unsophisticated?

Well, Father, I want the world to see You in me, so I am trying to overlay my soul with Your words, Your truths, Your actions. You know…Your gold. I'm trying to be…like You.

Ah, child, therein lies your error. This is the season to put away that wearying, gold-plating process you have been engaged in, and let Me scrape off the thin veneer you have been trying to present to the world. This is the year you are going to walk out your life with the silver part of you (your redeemed soul) on the outside, showing the world the vulnerable, tender, human, real you.

It will be painful, awkward, embarrassing, lonely, hilarious, exciting, and freeing. It will be refining and redemptive. You will be a living, breathing, walking, stumbling, falling, crying, laughing, failing, overcoming, loving example of silver being refined by My power, not yours. What I am aiming at, in you, is Me…the 100% Pure Gold. I want you to let Me turn you inside out!

Oh Father, I feel like weeping. I am amazed by Your love for me and by the knowledge that You are calling me to walk deeper with You. I am wary because I have not walked this particular path with You before, in this depth; but I'm excited, too. I know it will be painful to face the sources of my pride and my idols, in all their ugliness, as they fight to survive; but I also know that You will be with me in every battle.

You who have begun a good work in me will complete it, and the glory of my latter temple will be greater than the former. Until then, Father, and afterward, *Your praise shall continually be in my mouth* as *I make my boast in You* because I know, Lord, when the war clouds have cleared, I will, by Your love, grace, and power, come forth, refined and labeled as *simple, direct, and unsophisticated…100% Pure Gold.*

Let Your work begin!

Slow Down

Help me breathe and learn to know
That life is You and not a show.
Help me rest and slow the pace,
Receive Your love and taste Your grace.

So, You Want to Be a Fisherman?

"I want to be a fisherman," said the small boy to his dad.
"Then you must do the things I say," was his answer to the lad.

"Will you become fishers of men?" said Jesus to His crew.
"Then leave your father, ship, and nets. Come, do the things I do."

"You must be very patient, son, while you wait for fish to bite,
And often the best time to fish is in the dark of night."

"Sometimes, men, when the way is dark, and storm clouds start to roll,
Be patient, it may be the time to catch a hurting soul."

"You'll need the right equipment, lad: tackle, and fishing pole,
Sinkers, bobbers, hooks, and weights, and a good fishing hole."

"Truth, faith, peace, and righteousness is the armor you must wear.
Go ye unto all the world; lost souls are everywhere."

"Be quiet, boy, no need to shout, you'll scare the fish away.
Remember, too, that fish are fish no matter what they weigh."

"Be gentle as you speak the word to people everywhere,
And show them all, that big or small, God's tender love they share."

"So, my son, if an 'A-1' fisherman you would be,
Remember all I've said to you, and you'll be just like me."

*"So, if you want to follow the blessed Three in One,
Obey, and you will be conformed to the image of the Son."*

Sorrowful, Yet Always Rejoicing

Today as I sit quietly in my porch swing
Tearful sorrow at my side
I hear the steady splash of raindrops
Upon the roof
And yet at the same time
Through the rumbling thunder
Of the storm
I hear the lilting song of birds

Songs and sorrow
Tears and joy
Both needful
Both from You Lord
Both making me strong

May I learn,
As I walk in the storm
To always listen for the song of the bird.

...sorrowful, yet always rejoicing.

(II Corinthians 6:10)

Spell Blessing

"Spell BLESSING," said the Teacher as He surveyed the crowd.
"M-O-N-E-Y," replied the banker very proud.

"A-W-A-R-D-S." boomed the athlete standing tall.
"Blue ribbons, plaques, and medals to hang upon my wall."

"F-A-M-E," cooed the actress, flashing tooth-filled smile.
"Distinctions, Emmys, Oscars would make my life worthwhile."

"A-T-T-E-N-T-I-O-N," would solve my wishes,"
Cried the housewife overwhelmed with diapers, kids, and dishes.

"F-R-E-E-D-O-M!" the runaway did shout.
"To live my life the way I want is what it's all about."

"W-O-R-T-H," cried the woman of the street.
"I look for it within the arms of every man I meet."

"W-I-S-D-O-M," proudly spelled the scholar.
"Pursuit of it is of more worth than this world's mighty dollar."

Sadness filled the Teacher's face; a tear ran down His cheek.
His eyes swept o'er the silent room, not a soul dared speak.

And then an aged voice was heard from somewhere in the back.
An old man stood on feeble legs, wrinkled, shabby, black.

"J-E-S-U-S," he sang, for all the room to hear.
"THAT spells BLESSING," said the LORD, "and is music to My ear."

Sweet Sleep

*A*re you going through or have you ever gone through a period in your life when you find you are having difficulty sleeping? You either have trouble falling asleep or you fall asleep immediately, only to awaken in the early morning hours to stare at the ceiling until it is time to get up. If you have never experienced this, then praise God. But if you have battled sleepless nights, I would like to share something the Lord has shown me.

Psalm 127:2 declares that God gives His beloved sleep. Now I happen to believe I am one of His *beloveds*. So, if I am one of His *beloveds*, and He gives His *beloveds* sleep, why do I, at times, suffer these dozing dilemmas?

As I was pondering this puzzling question, I came upon Jeremiah 31:25 in which God proclaims He will *fully satisfy* the weary and *replenish* every sorrowful soul.

When studying the scriptures, I often look up definitions of certain words to expand what I know of their meaning. The word *satisfy* caught my attention. *Satisfy* means to make happy, to please, to gratify to the full. But the definition that caused my spirit's eye to take notice was the one that said: *to carry out the terms as of a contract.*

Wow! God says He will carry out the terms of contracts He has made with me! Just what contracts has He made? I began to make a mental list, then realized, very quickly, I could simply open His word and find them everywhere. He not only says He will carry out those contracts (promises), but that He will carry them out *fully*! He has made a contract with my weary soul, (and my soul feels extremely weary when confronted with night after night of sleeplessness.) So, this, to me, is encouraging news!

His contract says He will *replenish* my soul. *Replenish* means to supply fully, to fill with inspiration and power, to nourish, to build up again, to fill, to make full, to fill up again. Also encouraging news!

I continued reading Jeremiah 31:26 which says: *Upon THIS I awakened and beheld; and my sleep was sweet in the assurance it gave me.* Upon THIS I awakened? Upon THIS? What is the THIS I will awaken upon? The THIS in verse 26 is what God has promised in verse 25…a satisfied and replenished soul, also known as, sweet sleep. So, if I truly believe verse 25, then I will live out, experientially, verse 26.

Oh, beloved, I believe if you and I will meditate, memorize, ponder, and pray on verse 25 in Jeremiah 31 as we lay upon our beds, we will experience verse 26 in the morning. We will awaken and see that we have been beholding the Lord's promises before our spiritual eyes all night long. Holy Spirit will have filled our souls with assurance from God's precious, living Word, and our sleep will have, indeed, been *sweet.*

So, dear child of God, I bless you tonight. Rest easy in His arms of love, knowing He can be trusted to keep His contract. Close your eyes, and in the morning, *awaken beholding THIS…* you will have been *fully satisfied and replenished* as you experienced *His sweet sleep*

Taste Them Again for the Very First Time

I John 5:7 says: *There are Three who bear witness in heaven to the truth that Jesus is the Son of God. They are: the Father, the Word, and the Holy Spirit; and these Three are One.*

One morning, the reading of these words sent a jolt through my soul as Holy Spirit recalled to me a truth that, over time, had been pushed to the back of one of my heart's filing cabinet drawers—the truth that *Jesus is the Word.*

Of course, I knew that. Wasn't I quite adept at quoting John 1:1 and 14? *In the beginning was the Word and the Word was with God and the Word was God…and the Word was made flesh, and dwelt among us…*

It was not a *new* thought to me. It was what some would refer to as a *now* thought. At that particular moment I saw it as a re-*Newed Now* thought…somewhat like that old cereal commercial, 'Taste them again for the very first time.' I love that slogan because it describes what we, as Christians, can experience daily as we open our Bibles and let the life-giving words trickle into our souls like a healing balm. We read old familiar words that come alive and lead us into new revelations about God, Jesus, the Holy Spirit, ourselves, and others. We 'Taste them again for the very first time.'

God's word never ceases to amaze me, and I pray this amazement never ceases.

Have you ever thought or said these words? "If I could just hear God speak to me personally, then I could, more quickly, obtain:
*peace in a situation
*faith to believe for healing
*strength to face hard trials
*courage to trust that He will meet my needs
*patience to deal with life's daily irritations
*ad infinitum."
Maybe you haven't thought these thoughts; but I have, and I've thought them too many times I'm sorry to say.

So, therefore, when Holy Spirit spoke, with the gentleness only He can exude, I listened. "My child, you *can* hear God speak to you personally. Read I John 5:7 again."

I did. Amazingly, I heard and understood a little more clearly! JESUS IS THE WORD!

Holy Spirit spoke a second time "Read I John 5:7 once more."

And suddenly, as I read, I *tasted those words again for the very first time*. My understanding of them became even more clear. It was almost as if I had never read them before. I re-wrote them on my heart, this time in capital letters. GOD, THE WORD, AND THE SPIRIT ARE ONE!

These next words rolled into my heart very slowly.

Every. time . I. open . my . Bible . and . read . the . words . on . the . pages . inside, it . is . actually . Jesus (who.IS.the.Word) talking . to . me! And . since . the . Three . are . One. I . am . also . hearing . God . Himself (through.the.Holy.Spirit.living.in.me) speaking . to . me!

OH WOW! SELAH! (Stop and think about that!) I did. And I am still pondering the wonder of it!

In conclusion, dear ones, perhaps to *you* these NOW words to *me*, may seem like old stuff. Perhaps they strike *you* as a 'DUH-didn't-you-already-know-that?' familiar truth. But, at that particular moment, *I* was **tasting them again for the very first time...** and they were delicious!

 Ten Cent Sermon

s I was ending my morning walk with a five-minute, cool-down stroll, I noticed a dime on the sidewalk. It wasn't mine, plus it was covered in dirt, so I decided to leave it for someone else to claim. After all, it was only a dime, hardly worth the energy it would take to stoop down and pick up.

Several steps later I was brought to attention by the gentle nudging of Holy Spirit. "If that had been a quarter or a dollar, would you have picked it up?" He asked. I slowed down so I could listen more clearly. (I'm learning to recognize His nudges.)

"Well, probably," I answered.

"Ah, so you would have taken the time and energy to bend over and pick up a quarter because it's worth more. Is that correct?"

"I guess you could say that," I admitted. (I wondered where He was going with this. I could almost see Him smiling)

"I don't suppose this is going to be a lesson about money, is it?" I asked hesitantly.

"No, it's not going to be a lesson about money. It's going to be a lesson about WORTH."

I didn't answer, and He continued. "God happens to think dimes are important. He even thinks pennies are important. Do you think pennies are important?"

"No, not always," I confessed. "I suppose I should, but to be honest I don't. (I've learned it's a good idea to be honest when I'm talking to Holy Spirit).

"So then, if you lost a penny or a dime, you wouldn't search as diligently for them as the woman in the Bible searched for her lost gold coin, is that right?"

"Uh, yes, Lord, I guess that's right," I whispered.

Suddenly, a *God-moment* exploded in my soul! How many times had I passed by someone I deemed unworthy of the time and energy it would take to stoop down and lift them up?

I bowed my head in shame. "Oh Lord, forgive me for all the many times I've judged someone's worth by the world's standard of measurement, for all the times I've felt it would take too much energy or time to stoop and lift up someone I have considered to be one of the 'dimes' of life."

I quickly turned to retrace my steps keeping my eyes on the path, but saw no dime. "This is impossible," I muttered. "I know I saw a dime." Had I missed my opportunity to pick up that dime?

"Oh, Lord, how many opportunities have I lost because of my world's-eye view of worth? How many times, in my pride, have I marched blindly by what I considered a *lowly dime?*"

His next words pierced my heart, "He who has done it for the least of these has done it for Me."

Suddenly, there at my feet, was the dime. "Oh, thank You, Father," I cried as I looked at the now precious dime. "Please, Lord, help me to not pass by any more *dimes* because I consider them not worth my time and energy."

Then I heard His gentle voice, "My child, you were blind, but now do you see that what's done for the least is done for Me?"

"Yes, Father, I was blind, but now I do see. You're right. All are precious in Your eyes. People aren't just a *dime a dozen.*"

As I stooped to pick up the dime, I'm pretty sure I heard God chuckle.

That's What I Think

offee belongs in a mug. Wine belongs in a stemmed goblet. Hot tea belongs in a delicate china cup. Milk belongs in a 'glass' glass.

That's what I think.

Coffee would look ridiculous in a stemmed goblet. Wine most certainly should never be presented in a mug.

Hot tea served in a glass…I think not! Milk in Tupperware, well, it's just not right.

That's what I think.

Long pause…new thought enters.

Isn't it interesting that Jesus, the *New Wine*, is poured into various types of containers?

I ponder.

Would it be any less *New Wine* if it flowed forth from a not-so-handsome, or not-so-talented, or not-so-famous, or not-so-witty vessel?

More pondering.

Humm…another thought haughtily makes its appearance.

The *New Wine* belongs in a vessel worthy of it. It would look and taste much better. One would drink it in more willingly if poured from the proper container.

That's what I think.

Longer pause…silence…then a still, small voice.

Man looks on the outward appearance, but God looks on the heart.
(I Samuel 16:7)

THAT'S WHAT GOD THINKS!

Oh Father, forgive me! Please pass me a *mug of Wine.*

The Chair

Dedicated to my friend, Lisa

Kneeling by her kitchen chair,
A holy altar used for prayer,
The Word drops gently at her feet,
"Take your friend to the Retreat."

"But, Lord, she's paralyzed You know,
Confined to a chair; she cannot go.
I'd be a prisoner of that chair;
She would require my constant care."

"My child, I know just how you feel,
To talk with her you'd have to kneel,
Become a servant on bended knee;
Just like My Son you'd have to be."

"But why me, Lord?" He hears her say.
"She would need help both night and day."
"I know," He says, His voice not terse.
"That's why I'm choosing you...a nurse."

And though she seldom gets away
From high chairs, home, and kids at play,
With servant heart, she makes her choice,
Quietly heeds her Father's voice.

She spends her weekend by that chair
Feeding, dressing, showing care.
While others smile, hold doors, and nod,
She humbly serves a child of God.

Kneeling there she does not know
The power of God that gently flows.
To those who see that Holy chair,
She is an "angel" unaware.

As I watched my friend at the Ladies' Retreat ministering the love of Jesus to her new friend, my heart was so touched. I felt as if I were watching 'Jesus in action.' The retreat speaker may have had the attention of the audience, but she had the attention of the angels. I wrote this poem for and about my friend; and would, one day, love to read it before all the host of heaven as she receives her reward from our Father for being a good and faithful servant. Thank you, Lisa, for showing us Jesus 'with skin on.'

The Day a Hush Fell Over Hell

As demons gathered from afar,
Hell was filled with great elation.
The Son was dead! So, they rejoiced
In jubilant celebration.

They'd heard His cry upon the cross.
They'd seen the blood-stained spear.
They thought their victory was complete
Until the Son of God appeared.

A hush fell over hell that day
As Jesus walked through the door.
Satan's plan had gone up in smoke;
Over man, he would rule no more.

He had thought his task accomplished
And his kingdom finally begun,
But Satan had been defeated.
Jesus Christ, the Savior, had won!

Hallelujahs rang through heaven
As God's earth with praises did swell;
But down below, not a sound was heard…
The day a hush fell over hell.

The Much Mores
of My Heavenly Father

I love the writings of Oswald Chambers. I'm often tempted to think his intelligence and spiritual insights are too deep for me, but then I smile in amazement as Holy Spirit opens the eyes of my understanding, and I see exactly what God is saying to me through his words.

After pondering one of his devotional writings, this truth slipped quietly into my mind: Every time I feel far away from the Lord and have faltered in my *faith-walk*, it's because I've thought I have known better than God what should be done about certain situations or people in my life. I've let worries take over my mind and forgotten the *much mores* of my Father.

Wow! When I don't believe the words my Father says to me in the Bible, I am impertinently and flippantly saying that I know more than God! How arrogant! Never before have I pictured myself as standing before Almighty God and insolently saying, "You are wrong about this one, Father. I believe, in this particular case, I know more than You do. I am better equipped to handle the situation. So, step aside...please. I've got this one covered."

I am horrified at this thought, but that is exactly what I am doing! No matter how I re- arrange those words or how sweetly I speak them, they are spiritually proud, brash, and insolent. And as the truth of my actual spiritual position when I doubt God slammed into my heart, I was undone. I bowed my head. My tears fell. My heart broke.

Oh, Lord forgive me. Help me to trust You...in everything... and always.

I know I have *faith* because the word says *God has dealt to every man (and woman) the measure of faith.* (Romans 12:3) But *Unbelief* hammers at me from every direction as I face unexpected and unwanted circumstances in my life.

Lord, help me to recognize that when I stand in doubt and unbelief watching the flood waters slowly rise around me that I am allowing my worries to make me forget the *much mores* of You, my heavenly Father. (Matthew 6:30)

God, I want to keep my eyes on You and Your *much mores.* My cry to You echoes that of the father in Mark 9:24 who wanted so much to believe for his son's healing...*Lord, I believe; help my unbelief!*

Suddenly a light dawned in my spirit as I remembered the special word my Father had led me to ponder, claim, and declare, a few days earlier:

You will keep her in perfect peace whose mind is stayed on You because she trusts in You. (Isaiah 26:3)

Thank You, Lord. I believe that pondering and putting into practice these encouraging words will help me experience much more of Your *much mores.*

(II Corinthians 3:11; Romans 5:20)

Thirty Days
of Thankfulness

Day 1: Today I am thankful for my godly mother, who daily models Christlikeness to me. BTW, Mom, I agree that when we all get to heaven, what a day of rejoicing that will be!....and no, I don't wanna stay here at home with my baby dolls anymore. (When I was about four years old, one day Mom said to me: Oh Kathy, won't it be wonderful when we all get to heaven?! This was my answer: I think I'll just stay here with my baby dolls.)

Day 2: Clean water - cold water to drink, hot baths in the winter, refreshing swimming pool water, and my favorite water... ICE in my drinks.

Day 3: Today I am thankful for a husband who understands me (often better than I understand myself) and loves me anyway. He supports me, encourages me, and hangs stuff on the walls for me.

Day 4: I am thankful for my excellent health. Over 45 years ago (Wow), God used the surgeon's hands to correct my heart defect. Medical technology is amazing, but without God's healing hand I know it wouldn't have been enough.

Day 5: I am thankful to know THE SOURCE of our Resource, our family-owned business. I'm grateful for God's blessings upon His business and our ability to provide jobs for others too.

Day 6: I am so thankful to live in the USA where I do have a voice in the choice of our leadership.

Day 7: So thankful that my youngest son has a job interview/prospect today. God is faithful! He received that job and eventually moved on to his current position which he really enjoys. He gets to travel a lot and expand his knowledge and skills.

Day 8: Thankful to have learned the order of ALL of the books of the Old Testament, as did many of my young friends in SPLASH, our children's program, at church. I am so thrilled to finally have this VERY useful knowledge.

Day 9: Today I am thankful for the ability to sleep without difficulty. I know so many who struggle with sleeping, and I can't imagine the difficulty they have coping throughout their day constantly tired.

Day 10: I am thankful for music. Though I can't carry a tune or play a single instrument, I love music! Music is an amazing *tool* I use to worship God, to lift my spirit, to quiet my soul, to bring joy to my heart, to bring fun to a moment, and to bring a skip to my step ('cause I sure can't dance either)

Day 11: I am so thankful for the service & sacrifice of Veterans, past and present, who secure the freedoms that we Americans enjoy. May they be extra blessed.

Day 12: I am thankful for my house. I am thankful that it is a "home", but I am thankful for the house itself. We have the perfect location in our city. Close to all the necessities but "in the country". Awesome privacy, but neighbors close enough. It is the perfect size for our family and thanks to my amazing interior decorator, my very own sister, it has our personal touch throughout.

Day 13: I am thankful for our food. I'm grateful to be able to open the 'fridge and find something to eat. May not be what everybody wants but there is food there. Praise God!

Day 14: I am thankful for Bible teachers who have a great passion for God's Word and the amazing ability of writing/sharing with others the "great & hidden things" God has revealed to them. I love how their added insight impacts my time with my Savior and stretches my understanding of His glorious love and power.

Day 15: I love my precious grandson! He is 15 now. I am so thankful for him. He has such a tender heart and loves God!

Day 16: I'm thankful for my car. It gets me all the places I need and want to go and there are lots of those lately. It hauls all my *peeps* and all my *stuff*.

Day 17: I am thankful for weekends-sleeping in, time with my husband, and a slower pace than weekdays.

Day 18: I am thankful for the visitors we had in church with us this morning. We also had 50 children in SPLASH. Yea, God!! Thankful for my helpers today.

Day 19: I am thankful for dear, close friends. The ones with whom I walk, eat breadsticks with cheese, (then walk some more), do Bible study, visit thrift stores, float in the pool, read books on the beach, go to concerts, and most importantly – share what's on our hearts with. God has given me wonderful friends.

Day 20: I am thankful for my maternal grandmother. She had amazing courage and an unending smile. From her I have learned a joy of cooking and eating, as well as a gentle independence. (Ok, hers was gentle; mine, not so much.) I'm also thankful for my paternal grandmother. She had a quiet, gentle spirit and never failed to let me know I was loved. From her I received my blonde hair and smaller frame. She modeled *minimalism* which I captured and taught me to love frozen, iced oatmeal cookies.

Day 21: I am thankful for my first-born son. He is a hard -working, responsible, disciplined, tender-hearted young man. He is a loving daddy and wonderful provider for his son. Thank you, God, that You have preserved his life and that You WILL fulfill your purpose for him.

Day 22: I am thankful for our youngest son. He is strong-willed, confident, smart, adventurous, and has a great sense of humor. He plays ball, jumps on the trampoline, shoots Nerf guns and wrestles with his nephew. He is a wonderful uncle. It is good to see God molding this new heart of flesh in him.

Day 23: I am thankful for my Bible. God's living, breathing Word to me. It has brought salvation to my soul, healing to my body, comfort in sorrow, hope in despair, wisdom in times of uncertainty, and peace in troubling times. Daily His Word guides my walk here on this earth. It is powerful and true!

Day 24: I am thankful for the sandy beach of Daytona beneath my feet, the smell of freshly cut grass, a strong foot massage, the sign 'Terre Haute next 2 exits' after I've been away, and laughter that brings tears.

Day 25: I am thankful for songs that can take me back to special places/times in my life, Coke Icees, amazing Niagara Falls, flip flops, and good water pressure

Day 26: I am thankful for electronic banking, warm breadsticks with cheese, Sleeping Bear Dunes, painted toenails (mine, that is) and a cracklin' hot fire to toast my feet, Pinterest, curling irons, and pictures of my family and friends.

Day 27: I am thankful for my childlike faith. I know that I know that I know my Redeemer lives, and He lives in me. He was, is, and is to come-sooner as opposed to later, I hope. I can trust Him no matter what. He is faithful to ALL of His promises.

Day 28: I am thankful for the change of seasons. While spring and summer are my favorites, and I don't love bitter cold weather and the dreary brown of winter, I still enjoy change. I get to change my wardrobe and my furniture gets changed (rearranged) too. (Good thing we don't sleepwalk.)

Day 29: I am thankful for the many pets we have had over the years. They add such joy to our family. I remember Sunny, Clyde, Comet, Asia and the numerous kitty cats that have called our family theirs. Too bad those cats don't know better than to climb waaaayyy up in those trees. Sorry, kitties, Brian reached his limit after cutting down the second tree to save one of you.

Day 30: I am most thankful that I am blessed because I love and respect THE LORD and find great delight (health, protection, freedom) within the boundaries of His commands. My children will be mighty in the land and I am thankful. Surely, I will never be shaken. I will have no fear of bad news; my heart is steadfast, trusting in the Lord. My heart is secure in the palm of His hand. I will have no fear, and at the end of my life I will look in triumph over my foes (troubles/ heartaches of this world) and I will be forever THANKFUL!

Written by my daughter, Kathy Cottom. And oh, how it warms my heart every time I read it.

Trophies for God

As I look at the windows of our neighbors' den and see all the trophies lined up on the shelves proudly displaying their sons' victories on the tennis court, I smile. In my mind's eye I am trying to picture God's den and all the shelves He must need to hold His trophies.

I had just finished reading II Corinthians 2:14 in the Amplified Version of the Bible. It tells me that I sit on God's shelf as a trophy of Christ's victory.

Jesus Christ won me in the *battle* at the *Cross* which played out on Calvary before God Almighty and all creation. His triumph resounded throughout heaven, earth, and hell.

Death had lost and Life had won. Victory was His. I was the prize!

So the next time I am tempted to listen to the devil's lies that tell me I am a failure…a loser…a nobody, I'll just pay a little visit to my heavenly Father's den and take a look at what is standing proudly on the third shelf, second from the right.

Yep, that's me! There I am, all shiny and gold! I am God's trophy!

Turn Around and See

*...Behold, a woman, which was diseased with an issue of blood twelve years, came behind Him and touched the hem of his garment: For she said within herself, If I may but touch His garment, I shall be whole. Jesus **turned around, and seeing** her, He said, "Take courage, Daughter, be of good comfort..." (Matthew 9:20-22)*

Today, while reading these scriptures, I paused as I came upon the words uttered by the woman who had suffered with the issue of blood for so long. She said, *"If I can only touch His garment, I shall be whole."* But the following words describing what Jesus did *after* she had actually come up behind Him and touched the hem of His garment grabbed hold of my pondering place and wouldn't let go. *Jesus **turned around and seeing her** said, "Take courage, daughter, be of good comfort..."*

I began to ponder the determination of that dying woman. She knew that if she could just touch His garment she would be healed. I believe, though, that deep down inside what she really wanted to do was to touch His **actual body**. Perhaps just a slight touch of His arm or hand. She knew He had something she needed. He had the power of Almighty God residing in His **body**, and she wanted to touch it.

Why then did she decide to only touch His garment? Perhaps she felt she wasn't important enough or had the strength to get close enough to actually touch His physical **body**. Whatever the reason, she felt that if she could touch the closest thing to the very person of Jesus Himself, His garment, it would be enough.

Then God spoke these words to my heart, "My child, how many dying people at this very moment would love to be able to touch the power of God that resided in the **actual body** of Jesus so they could be made whole?"

"Thousands, Father," I answered, "but Jesus is no longer walking here on the earth in His fleshly **body**."

"Ah, but don't you find it amazing that He calls you, the Church, His **body**? He calls you, the people of God, His **body** on the earth today?"

As the revelation of what Holy Spirit was actually asking me took root in my heart, tears flowed as I began to ask myself the following questions:

Does the **body** of Christ, like Jesus, *turn around and see*?

Do we **turn around and see** those who are bleeding to death, or are we so focused on our own goals and ourselves that we can't feel the touch of the dying ones?

Are we moving so quickly toward our 'calling' that we don't take the time to **turn around and see** those who need a touch, but can't keep up with our pace?

Are we running so far ahead of Holy Spirit that all we feel is the wind in our faces and the hem of our garments flapping in the breeze…too unavailable to **turn around and see** the desperate needs of others?

Are we so busy that we can't **turn around and see** and feel the woundedness of others or hear their cries?

Are we too focused on the so-called 'important' tasks and people before us? Has our alleged 'self-importance' clouded our ability to **turn around and see** the hurt and anguish of those we might consider 'less important'?

What is it that stops us from slowing down to encourage and comfort those who are struggling to reach out and simply touch the **body** of Christ so that they might be made whole?

Oh, Church, **body** of Christ, for the love of God, let us begin to **turn around and see**!

Walk Bold and Brave

esterday I bumped into these words: *Walk bold and brave.* They grabbed me and held on. I knew, in my heart, that this was my *word* for the new year. This was the *word* God wanted me to concentrate on and walk out in my life, and I so longed to do it! When trouble came, I wanted to be found courageous and full of faith, but how would I perform the practicality of walking out this desire of my heart?

I had spent all of the previous year pondering and trying to flesh out these words: *Wherever you are...be ALL there.* Most days I had failed-big time, but there were other days I was happily surprised to find I was slowing down, being still, seeing, and hearing God. I was actually living in the 'now.' I was being ALL there. I hadn't done it nearly as often as I had wanted to, but I had done it more than I had before. I had spent the year trying to give my full attention to whatever I was experiencing. I had also practiced trying to give thanks to the Lord during those 'wherever I was' moments.

As I began to ponder the new year, I wondered how I could, in actuality, walk bold and brave when I knew that deep down inside I was a 'scaredy cat', a 'Chicken Little.' I am not at all bold and brave in the natural. Then I heard Holy Spirit say, "But all of you is not 'in the natural!' Part of you is SUPER-natural! Your Spirit is bold and brave even if your soul and body isn't." With this thought stampeding through my brain, I determined it was time for my soul to seriously begin to learn to operate in this truth. Then, together with my Spirit, perhaps the two of them could bring my body in line. I would then become a living, breathing example of *walking bold and brave*. Ah, good plan, but where do I begin?

First of all, to walk *bold* means I would have to walk in truth. I would have to see who I really am on the inside, acknowledge it, and be *bold* enough to willingly walk through my days being honest and real. No more being who I think I should be depending on wherever I am or whoever I am with. Being the real me regardless of the 'wherevers' and the 'whoevers'. It would mean walking in truth. Gulp! That, for me, would be walking *bold*, since I am a recovering people pleaser.

Secondly, to walk *brave* means I would have to put all of my trust in the Lord. *All* of it. No more listening to my natural wisdom. No more heeding the voices in the world telling me what they perceive to be the correct way to *flesh out* my *bravery*. No more leaning on my own strength, doing my own thing, until I realize it isn't working, and then turning to God.

To *walk bold and brave* would mean listening constantly to God's voice and believing He could be trusted. Trusted when my world is falling apart, whether in one big explosion or quietly eroding one tiny piece at a time. Trusted when there seems to be no way out. Trusted when no one sees my lonely, weary heart. Trusted when there seems to be no glimmer of hope in the discouragement surrounding me. Trusted when I feel as if I cannot even move, never mind walk. Trusted when I am not feeling *bold* or *brave*.

How can I trust and *walk bold and brave* when I can't even move? When I'm standing in the HARD?

Suddenly God's word broke through, and He brought it all home. "Haven't I commanded you to be strong and courageous? Would I tell you to do something you couldn't do? Don't be afraid or dismayed. I am your Lord, and I will always be in your 'wherevers.' Trust Me. Simply take that first fear-filled step, and you will discover you have taken the first step toward *walking bold and brave*." (Joshua 1:9; Deuteronomy 33:27.)

As the hands of the clock bring in a New Year,
Remember, My child, there is nothing to fear.
Walk bold and brave through trouble and tear.
Trust Me. Step forward...I will always be here.

Walking Wounded

We do not really see him as we pass him on the street.
Perhaps he's stooped and nondescript, slightly shuffles
with his feet.
We do not hear his story that is aching to be told.
We are running much too fast…no time for one who's old.

We do not see the once young man who left children,
home, and wife
To defend our country's freedom so we could chase our
dreams in life.
We do not feel the loneliness, the fear that crept at night,
The friends he lost, the tears he shed; yet still he stood to fight.

We hurry past this nameless face; someone we do not know.
So clueless, shallow, unaware of the debt to him we owe.
This gentle warrior shuffles by, no outward scars; and yet
He's walking wounded, deep inside, because the world forgets.

*Thank you for your years of sacrifice, my gentle warrior. I love you and
I do remember.*

(This was written for my husband, Bill, and the thousands of veterans who have served our country.)

Wayward Son

I see you there, my wayward son
Who walks no more with God.
Your fists are clenched,
My heart is wrenched
As I see the path you trod.

If I could hold you in my arms
The way I used to do,
I'd bring you home,
No more to roam
From the God that you once knew.

But time stands still for no one, son,
And babies become men.
So, while you stray,
I'll hope and pray
'Til you're back with God again.

I have a hope within my heart,
A hope that brightly burns,
That you won't wait
Until it's too late...
We wait for your return.

What Does God Require of Me?

What does God require of me?
Take a lesson from the tree.
Lift your arms up to the Son,
Share your fruit with everyone,
Take in nourishment,
Plant roots deep.
When storm clouds come
His strength you'll reap.

Psalm 1

What Have I Been Busy With?

hen attempting to reach the top of a staircase, I do not have to tackle the entire staircase all at once. I simply have to place one foot on the first step. In other words, I only need to take the first step. This, I believe, can apply to my walk of faith or my *staircase climb to heaven*. I don't have to tackle the whole staircase at once. I just have to take the first step in faith.

Although math is not my forte, I calculate that if I live to be one hundred, I am getting pretty near the top step of the staircase leading toward my final Home. (Home being the actual arms of Jesus.)

As I contemplated the unbelievable (at least to me) fact that I am old, I decided that although I am no longer considered even late-middle-aged, I am not yet ready to jump off the staircase and into an elevator taking me to my final destination. I want to run (well, maybe not run, but walk briskly) up that staircase until I have finished my race. I would rather fall into my Savior's arms, huffing and puffing, than walk into them from a stuffy elevator...spiritually speaking.

I don't want my faith to simply wear out, I want it to burn out from overuse. (OK, I know it is impossible for faith to burn out, but I think you know what I mean.) I want to see more salvations, more healings, more deliverances, more prosperity, more hope, love, joy, peace, more of everything in the kingdom of God before I step on that very last step of the staircase leading me Home! (And besides, how could I see all those wonderful things happening from inside the confines of an elevator.)

II Corinthians 5:10 in the Amplified Bible spells out some of the things I will be asked when I stand before the judgment seat of God. The one question that stands out to me today as I sit pondering on my porch swing is this: *What have I been busy with?* I know what I want my answer to be. I want to be able to say, "Father, all the way up the staircase I have been busy being about *Your* business." But, in all truthfulness, I can't say that because, more often than not, I have been busy being about *my* business and not *His*.

As I was asking myself how I could better go about being busy, not with *my* business, but with *His* for the last few steps up the staircase, Holy Spirit reminded me of something I had read years ago. A believer doesn't just listen to the word of God. A believer *acts* on it. A believer does what God tells her to do and then believes God will do what He says in His word that *He* will do. For example: Noah built the ark, but God brought the flood; Joshua marched around the walls of Jericho, but God made them fall down; Believers pray and lay hands on the sick, but God makes them well. God tells us to do what we can do, then He does what only He can do.

I suddenly realized I had my answer about how to *be about my Father's business* for the rest of my staircase journey. God's mandate, not to me alone, but to all of us is this: Today, whatever we face, just take the first step in faith. We don't have to see the whole staircase. We just have to listen to God, go into the world, take that first small step, give what we have, and let God anoint it. If we do this, we will find ourselves busy *being about our Father's business* and not our own.

Whispers from God

Sunday, while driving to church, I was being most careful to obey the speed limits. As I was nearing my destination, I suddenly realized I had gradually been accelerating and was now speeding along quite merrily. "Oh dear," I thought, "it would be terrible to have obeyed the traffic laws all along the way only to receive a speeding ticket for disobeying them just before I had reached my destination."

I immediately felt an incoming message from God whispering to my heart: "You know, My dear, this little example applies to my people and their walk in my kingdom. I tell my people to OBEY My laws and, like you, they often break them just before they arrive at their final destination.

I tell them to OBEY My laws/My words no matter where they are or what their circumstances might be as they face their problems in life.

I tell them to OBEY Me when I implore them in My word to bring all their worries and cares to Me in prayer, to leave them with Me, to believe that I am GOD, that I am in control, and that I will take care of them.

I don't *only* tell my people to OBEY Me. I also tell them to TRUST Me.

I tell them to TRUST My words that tell of My love for them as they face their trials.

I tell them to TRUST Me when I say I am with them always and will never leave them.

But, too often, as they near their destination, they forget My words. They become weary in obeying...in trusting...in well-doing...in praying...in believing...in hoping...in looking up...in letting Me be God. They give up! When they give up, they disobey My words, break My laws, and break My heart.

Will you tell them not to become weary in their obedience to Me? Will you tell them to hold on to their trust in My promises to them?

Will you tell them how My heart breaks as I watch those who have been trusting and obeying all along their journey only to become disobedient as they draw near their final destination because they have forgotten My love for them and My desire to be a very present and well-proved help in all of their circumstances?

Will you tell My people to OBEY Me and TRUST Me? To OBEY Me by giving their worries and fears to Me in prayer? To TRUST Me by believing I will do what I say I will do?

Will you tell My people to HOLD ON? To not GIVE UP or GIVE IN or GIVE OUT? Will you tell them to OBEY My *traffic laws* all the way to their final destination?

Will you tell them for Me?"

Whose Report Will You Believe?

t this stage of my life I am choosing to pray and believe for healing until I see my friends and loved ones healed or actually Home in the arms of Jesus. I have determined not to become discouraged when God doesn't do things my way. I will continue to lift my eyes to the Lord, knowing that He is good *all* the time. His word is true no matter what I see or don't see, and He is trustworthy and full of loving kindness. If my prayers are not answered in the way I have hoped, I will fix my eyes on Jesus, continue to proclaim His awesome faithfulness, and prepare to fight the next battle against the enemy.

I would like to share with you what I believe the Lord spoke to me one morning as I was praying for my friend who had received a 'bad report' from the doctor. She was battling discouragement and depression. Even though I knew she would be victorious in the end, I also knew it is the daily battle that can be so wearying.

My heartfelt prayer was interrupted by these words from Holy Spirit: "Why is it that when my people hear one or two *reports* from a doctor or a medical test and then look at the *stacks* of *reports* I have given them in My word, they choose to allow discouragement to attack their faith? Why would one little *stack* of *reports* from man carry more weight in their position of faith than the hundreds of *stacks* of *reports* from My word?"

All I heard was the gentle squeaking of my porch swing as I wrestled with His words. I had no answer.

I began to read and ponder the incalculable number of *stack*s of His *reports* and then compare them to the scare tactics brought on by the teeny-tiny, pitifully-thin stack of the enemy's *reports*, and suddenly many of the areas of unbelief hiding in my soul were blown to *smithereens* by the truth bomb of His Holy Spirit.

There are many things I don't understand, but this I know: *I trust my God and His love for us, and I trust His word.*

I have now begun to pray with more confidence than ever before. I am determined that whenever discouragement begins to creep in as I pray for the healing of others, I will bring to my remembrance the picture Holy Spirit painted in my mind's eye of the enormous differences in the heights of those *stacks* of *reports*. I will remember the power of God's mighty promises in His *stacks of reports* compared to the powerlessness in the enemy's tiny *stack* of lies.

Praise God! I know, without a doubt,
whose report I am going to believe.

Will you join me?

You Still Have Mountains to Take

Those that are planted in the house of the Lord shall flourish in the courts of our God. They shall still bring forth fruit in old age; they shall be full of spiritual vitality and rich in trust, love, and contentment. (Psalm 92:13,14)

As I approached my 77th birthday, I was pondering whether or not it was time to think about slowing down, sitting back, settling in, and resting on my past laurels for the remainder of my years here on earth. After all, I reasoned, I am occasionally forgetful, sometimes out-of-step with the world today, and often tired. In other words, I am old!

I learned that God has other plans for us older saints as later that night I awoke from a deep sleep, fumbled for my bedside tablet and pen, and began to write the words He was speaking to my heart, "I want you to burn out, not wear out. You are never too old to serve Me. Don't get that mindset. You still have much to give and to share with others."

I then felt impressed to go into the living room. As I flipped on the light, my eyes were drawn to the bookcase, and I heard these words, "Do you see all those new shiny books lined up with their bright colorful covers? Pretty eye-catching, aren't they?"

"Oh, yes," I replied. "I love new books!"

"Now look at the old books. They are looking a bit drab and forlorn compared to the others, aren't they?"

"Yes," I replied a bit sadly.

"Well," God continued, "old books on the shelf may look and feel cracked, worn, and used-up, but they still hold *treasures* on the inside. If you settle in on the shelf, never to be used again, you will become dusty and musty-smelling. I want you in *circulation* so you will continue to send forth the fresh sweet aroma of Christ.

You have to give of the treasure inside yourself. Don't try to update it by putting on a new cover or rewriting the message in an attempt to reach today's audience. Simply give the precious, heart-carried message in the same familiar way you always have. It never grows old.

Don't try to be a new condensed version or a paperback. People often try to update old books and movies to fit the world's mold for today, but they never seem to be quite as good as the originals."

God then brought this example to my mind. My old Bible had begun to fall apart, so I bought a new one just like it (except it was large print). It was a nice Bible. It was a fine Bible. It was a new Bible. But, oh, how I hated to give up my old one. So much of my *life* with the Lord had been written inside that old book. I had made hundreds of notes in it as Holy Spirit had revealed truths to me over the years. It was worn, torn, and patched with tape on the outside, but that *precious* old book, now retired on a shelf, was *priceless* to me.

Then I heard God whisper, "That is exactly how I feel about you, My child, except I am not retiring you on a shelf. To others you may appear worn, torn, and patched, but to Me you are precious and priceless.

Paul said to Timothy: *Let no one despise your youth.* But I say to you:

Let no one despise your old age.
You are part of My Caleb Generation…

You still have mountains to take."

Acknowledgements

have so many people to thank for helping me to realize my dream of publishing a book. First of all, my kind-hearted husband, Bill, who over the years, has had these ponderings pounded into his ears as he became the sounding board for each finished piece of writing.

Without my precious daughters, Kim and Kathy, there would have been no book. Time and time again, they patiently came to the rescue of their overwhelmed, teary-eyed, computer-challenged mother.

I'm grateful for my dear sister, Judy, who encouraged me to step-it-up and finally finish my book and generously provided financial help in the publishing process.

I want to thank all my swing-sharing soul sisters who have pondered with me through the years. Special thanks to Janet and Cherie for their encouragement and many helpful suggestions.

My greatest thanks and gratitude go to my Father God who loves me, my Jesus who saved me, and the Holy Spirit, who is the true producer of all the *Ponderings from My Porch Swing.*

Peggy Purcell Hanna

About the Author
by the Author

This book has been written by a woman who loves to sit on her porch swing and ponder.

My name is Peggy, and I ponder…a lot. For years, I have wanted to write a book, so I decided to put my ponderings in a book to pass on to my children, grandchildren, great-grandchildren, relatives, friends, and anyone else I could coerce into meditating on my musings.

I am a born-again believer who loves Jesus with all my heart. Since becoming a Christian at the age of 26, I have been chasing hard after God every day. I am a wife, mother of three, grandmother of seven, and great-grandmother of two. (When my first "great" was born, I told everyone I was too young to be a great-grandmother, so they could just call me Nana the Great. They don't, so I'm just Nana to all of them.)

I am a sister, a friend, a retired elementary teacher, and a talker. (Oh, can I talk! I'm working on that, though. My goal is to one day be able to add the words *good listener* to my list.) I have been a Sunday School teacher, Vacation Bible School teacher, Children's Worship leader, Women's Ministry leader, Bible Study teacher, speaker at ladies' gatherings, and mentor.

For over fifty years, I've been a Bible-studier, a pray-er, a journaler, a laugher, a learner, and an avid reader. I love Christian books, biographies, and mysteries, but I love reading the Bible most of all.

I am also a hit-the-ball-drag-Peggy golfer, a YouTube sermon-listener, a Pinterest follower, and a 30-minutes-three-times-a-week treadmill walker (I call it the *dreadmill* because I don't love exercising.) But my favorite thing in all the world is to talk about Jesus to anyone who will talk back to me.

I am currently engaging in something I've never done before-I'm learning how to *be old*. One of the ways I'm practicing this new adventure is by spending more time on my porch swing: relaxing, reading, visiting with friends, pondering, and thanking God for loving me so much.

As you have read my ponderings, my heartfelt prayer is that something in them has touched your heart, your soul, or your funny bone and drawn you just a little bit closer to my Jesus.

Peggy Purcell Hanna

CPSIA information can be obtained
at www.ICGtesting.com
Printed in the USA
LVHW040833051020
667943LV00020B/456